The Great Reform Act
of 1832

Second edition

IN THE SAME SERIES

General Editors: Eric J. Evans and P.D. King

LANCASTER PAMPHLETS

The Great Reform Act of 1832

Second edition

Eric J. Evans

London and New York

First published in 1983 by Methuen & Co. Ltd

Reprinted 1988, 1991, 1992
by Routledge

Second edition published 1994
by Routledge
11 New Fetter Lane, London EC4P 4EE

Simultaneously published in the USA and Canada
by Routledge
29th West 35th Street, New York, NY 10001

Reprinted 2000

Routledge is an imprint of the Taylor & Francis Group

© 1983, 1994, Eric J. Evans

Typeset in 10 on 12 point Bembo by
Ponting–Green Publishing Services, Chesham, Bucks
Printed in Great Britain by
Clays Ltd, St Ives PLC

British Library Cataloguing in Publication Data
A catalogue record for this book is available from the British Library

Library of Congress Cataloging in Publication Data
Evans, Eric J.
The Great Reform Act of 1832/E.J. Evans. – 2nd ed.
p.   cm. – (Lancaster pamphlets)
Includes bibliographical references
1. Great Britain. Parliament–Reform–History–19th century.
I. Title.   II. Series.
JN543.E93   1994
328.3'042'094109034–dc20   94–17967

ISBN 0–415–11793–3

Contents

Foreword

Lancaster Pamphlets offer concise and up-to-date accounts of major historical topics, primarily for the help of students preparing for Advanced Level examinations, though they should also be of value to those pursuing introductory courses in universities and other institutions of higher education. Without being all-embracing, their aims are to bring some of the central themes or problems confronting students and teachers into sharper focus than the textbook writer can hope to do; to provide the reader with some of the results of recent research which the textbook may not embody; and to stimulate thought about the whole interpretation of the topic under discussion.

Preface to the second edition

The opportunity to produce a second edition of a text which has been widely used is a privilege which should not be abused. While it affords an opportunity to correct error and to clear up infelicities, it is not an excuse to write a different book. Several additions and other changes have been made to the original text, therefore, but I have retained most of its original structure.

Those familiar with the first edition, published as one of the six inaugural Lancaster Pamphlets in 1983, might appreciate knowing where emphases have been changed. In the first place, the Pamphlets have been encouraged to expand both in number and in length since 1983 and I have taken the opportunity to bring this Pamphlet nearer to the length of many of those published more recently. This extra scope has allowed opportunity for deeper investigation of certain important areas. It is clear, in the light of research published since 1983, that my treatment of the unreformed electoral system was both too monochrome and too uncharitable. I hope that I have corrected any impression which my earlier work might have given that all eighteenth-century voters were corrupt, venal and (at least by the end of the poll) thoroughly drunken. Only some were!

Second, I have given greater emphasis to the travails of Toryism at the end of the 1820s. It is at least arguable that the main reason why parliamentary reform was enacted in 1832 was not that many at Westminster feared imminent revolution (though many certainly did) but because the Tory party, that adamantine edifice against reform since the 1790s, became a divided, demoralized and indifferently led organization between early 1827 and late 1830 when it left office. Here I examine why. To make this discussion more manageable, I have created two chapters (Chapters 6 and 7), dealing with the periods 1820–30 and 1830–2 from the one in the first edition.

Third, I have expanded the final section to provide a clearer bridge between this Pamphlet and that written on the Second Reform Act by my colleague Dr John Walton in 1987 (20). Historians have disputed whether 'continuity' or 'change' should be the main theme in any treatment of the importance of the so-called 'Great Reform Act'. This enlarged section gives students more scope in which to come to their own conclusions, though they will note that the author has not repressed his own views on the subject!

Anyone who writes a Lancaster Pamphlet on a central examination topic soon finds his or her postbag swollen by invitations to address sixth-form conferences, undergraduate student societies and similar events. Such invitations are welcome since they help to bridge any gulf which might exist between school and university, scholar and student. It is also valuable for students to see that the authors whose texts they have wrestled to understand (not, they hope, to memorize!) and/ or the examiners responsible for the questions they attempt at A-level look at least passably normal, are capable of sharing a joke and are not otherwise impossibly distanced from a student world. Such interchanges are, in my view, both healthy and mutually beneficial since lecturers learn from them as well. Many of the fresh thoughts about parliamentary reform which have found their way into this new edition have had their origins on return journeys reflecting on questions asked at a conference or a student society meeting and responding to the interest and enthusiasm shown by audiences. Such ideas have (albeit often unwittingly) been shared with students at Lancaster on my return. I am immeasurably grateful for the various contributions made: more often than questioners or Lancaster students will realize, they have suggested a new angle or emphasis. It is often asserted that authorship is a solitary occupation. The *process* of writing inevitably is but the *product* is frequently a more collaborative business than readers realize. It is appropriate to end this Preface to a new edition with warm appreciation of the many contributions made to it by students as well as fellow scholars.

Lancaster, March 1994

Acknowledgements

My gratitude to the large number of students who have helped me refocus my thoughts for this second edition is noted in the Preface. I am grateful to Jessica Marquis for giving her time so generously to help me with layout, diagrams and the higher word-processing skills. Thanks are also due to my co-editor, Dr P. D. King, and to Dr J. A. Carr who read through the revised manuscript and who offered many helpful suggestions to aid clarity. I hope that, among many other valuable points, they have helped me to appreciate that long words are best placed in short sentences!

1

Introduction: then and now

On 7 June 1832 King William IV gave his royal assent to the first Reform Act. He had many misgivings about the wisdom of the measure and, pointedly, he refused to attend the House of Lords to give the assent in person. He also gave directions that public buildings were not to be illuminated and that no firework display was to be held to mark the event. The Act was passed as the climax to a two-year period of high political tension and excitement both within parliament and outside. Many MPs believed that, unless a measure of parliamentary reform were passed no later than the spring of 1832, a violent revolution would sweep away all established institutions. Chaos and bloodshed, such as the French had experienced forty years earlier during the 'Terror' phase of their revolution, would befall Britain.

The Reform Act was not a piece of timeless constitution-making, the product of a full and dispassionate consideration of the nation's needs. It was a compromise stitched together during a crisis. It dissatisfied a substantial majority of those who had most strenuously urged the need for parliamentary reform. Yet, from the government's point of view, it served its major purpose: it removed the immediate threat to the security of the state. In a broader context, too, the Reform Act deserves to be remembered as one of the most momentous pieces of legislation in the history of modern Britain. As its name implies, it was the first thoroughgoing attempt to redraw the political map and define which categories of persons should, and which should not, have the vote. Looked at from a modern perspective, 1832 can be seen as the vital first step on the road to full, representative parliamentary democracy. We know, though contemporaries could not, that the 1832 Reform Act was not destined to be, as Lord John Russell put it at the time, 'the final solution of a great constitutional question'. Further reforms were not so long delayed. Extending the vote to adult male householders in 1867 produced working-class majorities in many urban constituencies thereafter. The Third Reform Act (1884) produced a similarly modest male franchise threshold in rural areas, giving the vote to humble miners and many agricultural labourers. Virtually all men who had not qualified for the vote before 1918 were given it then, together – much more famously – with women ratepayers of 30 years and above. Full female suffrage from the age of 21 arrived in 1928. In 1969, the definition of voting 'adulthood' was changed to include virtually all people of 18 years and above, so that for the last quarter-century many people taking their A-level examinations at school have been entitled to vote in parliamentary and local elections.

The complement to extended voting rights was legislation to make elections fairer and less corrupt. Votes were cast in secret after 1872. In 1883, strict rules were introduced which governed election expenditure and proscribed undue 'influence' on voters. After 1885 parliamentary constituencies were to be of roughly equal size, and after 1948 every voter was restricted to a single vote, in a single constituency. Many would argue that the system created by this welter of legislation and regulation over the past century-and-a-half remains imperfect. Some see a 'first-past-the-post' system in single-member constituencies as less fair than one which rewards political parties in strict proportion to the total number of votes cast overall. Some have also maintained that a mass press, as popular as it has become vulgar, meretricious and mendacious, is disproportionately weighted on one side of the political fence and thus exerts inappropriate influence on the outcome of elections. The triumphalist headline from one such newspaper two days after the 1992 general election – 'It's the Sun wot won it!' – might be said to offend against more than the rules of grammar.

Despite any remaining faults, the electoral system operating at the end of the twentieth century offers much fairer and wider representation than that which the Whigs reformed in 1832 and this system can trace lineal descent from 1832. The reformers of 1832, however, would have been horrified at such an outcome. They believed, along with the great historian and Whig politician Thomas Babington Macaulay, that democracy was 'fatal to the purposes for which government exists'. Sir Robert Peel, who opposed the Reform Bill to the very last, but who then proved himself, first as leader of the major opposition party and then as prime minister, one of the best manipulators of the new system, rationalized his objections thus: 'I was unwilling to open a door which I saw no prospect of being able to close.'

The Reform Act, therefore, merits study not only for what it was, but for what it set in motion. Before scrutinizing the Reform Act and its immediate origins, this book will seek to explain how parliamentary reform came to be the central political issue of the age. Since plans for amending the constitution had been common since at least the 1760s it is also relevant to ask why the reformers had to wait so long to achieve a measure of success. The broader significance of reform will be examined in a final section.

2

The unreformed parliamentary system

How members came to sit in the House of Commons before 1832 was a haphazard business. Both the qualification to vote in a parliamentary election and the places which had the right to send members to Westminster depended very largely on custom and precedent. Parliamentary seats fell into two broad categories: county and borough. Appendix 3 shows their distribution. Only in the county seats is some uniformity found. Each English county sent two members to parliament, irrespective of its size or population. When elections were contested, the right of voting had since 1430 rested with men who owned freehold land or property to the value of at least forty shillings (£2). They cast two votes for the candidates of their choice in a single election; the *two* candidates with most votes, unlike the modern system, were declared elected. These 'forty shilling freeholders' in England and Wales could be men of very considerable substance or they might own little more than a cabbage patch. This was because the effects of inflation since the fifteenth century had rendered the qualification to vote much easier to achieve than was originally intended. Also, the definition of 'freeholder' was in the eighteenth century interpreted with increasing liberality. It frequently included those holding leases or mortgages and so might encompass even artisans or traders. As contemporaries recognized, however, the county electorate was rather more uniform and solidly respectable than its borough counterpart.

4

In Scotland, which sent members to the English parliament after the Act of Union in 1707, the right to vote was very much more restricted in both counties and burghs. Only property owners to the value of approximately £100 qualified and most electorates were very small. In 1831, when Scotland's population was 2,364,000 the total electorate was about 4,500. In the county of Bute, which then had a population of 14,000, only 21 electors voted for the two county members.

No attempt was made to link representation to the density of population. This appeared increasingly odd from the late eighteenth century when the industrial revolution was concentrating people in Lancashire, the West Riding of Yorkshire, Staffordshire and Warwickshire. Lancashire's population in 1831 was 1,337,000 yet it sent only two county MPs to Westminster; so did Rutland with a population of 19,000. The majority of English voters, about 55 per cent, voted in county seats despite the fact that only 16 per cent of England's seats were from the counties. The system was extremely hard to justify on rational grounds.

Most, if not all, of England's 203 parliamentary boroughs had been centres of population but some had not thrived since the thirteenth or fourteenth centuries when parliamentary status had been granted. Most had been county towns, market towns or seaports attracting a reasonable degree of commerce. In 1800, a few – Bristol, Coventry, Hull, Liverpool, Plymouth, Preston and, of course, London – remained important centres with rapidly expanding populations. In 1831 London and Liverpool were Britain's two largest cities. A large group, much smaller in population, remained respectable communities with an important range of administrative and mercantile functions. They included county towns like Bedford and Stafford and market towns like Ripon in Yorkshire or Bridgwater in Somerset. Most such communities had populations of 5,000 to 10,000.

It was against the third category of parliamentary borough that hostility was directed. These were places with very small populations and often declining economic functions. Some seemed redundant by 1800 for all purposes except providing two members of the House of Commons. Dunwich in the thirteenth century had been a Suffolk seaport of some note, but coastal erosion had put much of it into the North Sea, leaving 44 houses standing in the borough by 1831. The place had 32 electors for its two members. Old Sarum, two miles to the north of Salisbury, was so derelict that sightseeing tours were arranged to view the ditches and remains of a castle which were all that remained of the old community. Its eleven electors had last been called upon actually to vote in an election in 1715.

None of the Cornish coastal boroughs of Camelford, East Looe and West Looe, Newport, St Germans and St Mawes could muster a population of 1,000 in 1831, but together they placed twelve men in the House of Commons. Three of Surrey's six boroughs – Bletchingley, Haslemere and Gatton – were similarly empty and the last of these had only seven electors.

Thus, sparsely inhabited boroughs sent members to Westminster while many large industrial centres did not. Parliamentary representation entirely failed to keep pace with the shift in the balance of wealth and of population from south to north. In 1831, the cities of Manchester (population 182,000), Birmingham (144,000), Leeds (123,000) and Sheffield (92,000) had not a single MP between them. At the beginning of the nineteenth century, Cornwall with a population of 192,000 sent 44 members to parliament. Lancashire sent a mere 14. The southern bias was most notable. In 1801 the six English counties with a southern coastline (including the Isle of Wight) accounted for one-third of all England's MPs (162 out of 489; 150 borough seats, 12 county) though they contained only 15 per cent of its population.

The distribution of seats in parliament was one glaring anomaly in the old system; the right of voting was the other. The wide divergencies in borough voting qualifications were legendary. The system was enormously complex but boroughs may be broadly classified into five types: those in which any adult male who paid local poor rates could vote in an election (the so-called 'scot and lot' boroughs); those in which every resident male of at least six months standing who was not a pauper could vote (the 'potwalloper' boroughs); the 'burgage boroughs' in which voting rights were inherited, virtually as pieces of property; the 'corporation boroughs' in which members of the local corporation were the sole electors; and the 'freeman boroughs' in which the electors were those who qualified in various ways to be considered freemen. Most of the electorates in the first two categories were wide in late eighteenth-century terms, with more than 500 voters per borough. The third and fourth categories

6

were very small, with electorates usually less than 100. In the fifth category, since the definition of freeman could be interpreted widely or narrowly, both large and small electorates were found.

Defenders of the old system made a virtue of this diversity, arguing that it ensured the representation of a wide, though unequal, range of interests. They also argued that, since property rather than numbers had traditionally been the appropriate qualification for electoral representation, statistics about population growth in electorally under-represented areas were irrelevant.

Diversity certainly produced interesting effects. In some large boroughs almost all permanently resident adult males had the vote before 1832. Here, elections were frequent and public opinion at elections could be reliably gauged. In many of the largest boroughs, furthermore, electorates increased alongside growing populations – especially in the leading commercial and industrial areas – and more electoral contests were held between 1780 and 1831 than in the 40 years after the Hanoverian succession in 1714. To that extent, one of the central arguments of those who would oppose parliamentary reform in 1830–2 was valid: the old system *was* capable of change and adaptation to new circumstances. Westminster, for example, had a massive 12,000 electors on the eve of the Reform Act, making it far larger than virtually every new borough created from Midland and northern industrial England in 1832. Bristol, Leicester, Liverpool, Nottingham and Preston all had electorates of about 5,000 at the same time, while Northampton and Norwich were comfortably in four figures. On the eve of the Reform Act, the fourteen largest borough electorates numbered between them almost 71,000 voters – more than one-third of the voters from 417 English and Welsh borough seats as a whole. A very few county constituencies, such as Middlesex, were comparably large; Yorkshire, with 23,000 voters in the early nineteenth century, was the largest constituency of all. At the other end of the scale, tiny Rutland struggled to muster 800 voters.

Most boroughs had small electorates. It had been estimated that, in 1830, 43 of the 202 English boroughs had electorates in excess of 1,000 and 46 were between 300 and 1,000. Of the remaining 113, 56 were truly 'rotten boroughs' with fewer than 50 voters each. In very general terms, the smaller the number of electors, the less frequently those electors were actually required to cast a vote because the seat was controlled by a 'patron'.

Patronage was one of the keystones of unreformed British politics. Elections in many boroughs became unnecessary because constituencies were effectively the property of great landowners or of the crown. The voters might be tenants of the borough 'proprietor' or they might have financial or other inducements not to vote for any candidate other than the proprietor's nominee. An election, therefore, was a waste of time. No one would challenge a candidate nominated by Earl Fitzwilliam for the Northamptonshire borough of Higham Ferrers, for example, and no election was held there between 1702 and the borough's abolition in 1832. The two seats for Appleby (Cumbria) were shared between the Earls of Lonsdale and Thanet. Sir Philip Francis gave an amusing account of his selection there in 1802:

> I was unanimously elected by one elector to represent this ancient borough in Parliament . . . there was no other candidate, no Oppositon, no Poll demanded. . . . So I had nothing to do but to thank the said elector for the Unanimous Voice with which I was chosen. . . . On Friday morning I shall quit this triumphant Scene with flying Colours and a noble determination not to see it again in less than seven years.

Roughly half of Britain's MPs sat in Westminster because a patron had put them there. Since voting was an open declaration of allegiance and not a secret ballot, landowners could easily check whether electors defied them. It is not surprising that about one-fifth of all MPs were the sons of peers; their fathers feathered the family nest. Nor is it surprising that fewer than one-third of parliamentary seats were contested in the century before the Reform Act.

Even the avoidance of elections, however, was expensive. Borough patrons had to consider the material comforts of 'their' electors. 'Keeping up the interest' could cost a nobleman upwards of £5,000 during the course of a parliament. The Grosvenor family was alleged to spend £4,000 a year in the late eighteenth century to ensure continued control of the borough of Chester. Nearly all borough 'owners' were great landowners, though successful businessmen could buy their way to political influence via a seat in parliament. The price – between £4,000 and £6,000 at the turn of the century – deterred all but the most wealthy. Nevertheless, Bedford became the preserve of the Whitbread brewing family; Tamworth, in Staffordshire, was shared between the Marquis of Townshend and Sir Robert Peel senior, the cotton magnate from Bury, who used the borough to launch the political careers of his sons William and the future prime minister, Robert junior.

Influence did not of itself prevent contests from time to time; Bedford and Tamworth were both contested only once between 1800 and 1832 but elections could be ruinously expensive. Those fighting county seats in the eighteenth century might expect to lay out at least £3,000 to £4,000 each to cover electors' costs in travelling to the poll, their food, drink and often lavish entertainment. Only one polling station (usually in the county town) was available, so travelling expenses in far-flung counties such as Yorkshire, Lincolnshire or Devon were bound to be steep. The contested Yorkshire election in 1807 cost an unprecedented £250,000 in all – a quite stupendous sum. Even a by-election in a relatively small borough, such as Lincoln, cost £25,000 in 1808. Not surprisingly, several families were ruined by unwisely entering contests in which they were overmatched. A relatively uncontentious election could cost thousands of pounds. Many borough voters in the numerous Cornish seats required transport from their residences in London in order to cast their votes. There was no postal ballot. They would expect appropriate accommodation while away and adequate recompense to compensate for their temporary loss of the pleasures of the capital in a remote Celtic wilderness.

The poll itself, as the work of the artist Hogarth reminds us, was a boisterous if not a riotous affair. Affrays were frequent; the antics of rival groups of frequently intoxicated supporters bring vividly to mind the weekly romps of contending partisans in a more modern spectator sport. For the voters, and often for the town as a whole, an election was an event to be savoured. Not only did the candidates provide free beer, but a poll which lasted a couple of weeks to allow distant voters travelling time kept the drink flowing. Since open voting was practised, the drama of the contest was heightened. Candidates could check running totals and know which palms had yet to be greased, which absent voters cajoled to the poll. The whole business was pure, or perhaps more accurately impure, theatre. Two more pieces of evidence might be produced in support of the case that the eighteenth-century electorate was not only unrepresentative but was becoming more so. First, the number of voters in no way kept pace with the increase in population as a whole. The electorate at the time of the Glorious Revolution (1688–9) was about 240,000. It had increased to about 340,000 by the time of George III in the 1760s and 1770s. Thereafter, as population in most of the less controlled parliamentary boroughs increased sharply so the numbers entitled to vote grew more rapidly. O'Gorman estimates that the electorate was close to 440,000 on the eve of the Reform Act, having increased by about 83 per cent since the Glorious Revolution. Such a growth in what many persist in seeing as an ossified system is worthy of note. However, at the same time the population of England and Wales rose by about 155 per cent from approximately 5.5 million to 14 million. The proportion of adult males entitled to vote thus decreased substantially.

Second, the opportunities for that electorate actually to vote dwindled. During the reign of Queen Anne (1702–14) elections had to be held every three years under the terms of the Triennial Act (1694). In fact, they occurred even more frequently during what Professor J. H. Plumb has called 'the rage of party' between Whigs and Tories. After the Whigs had established overwhelming political dominance in 1715, they moved speedily to take both the heat and, if possible, the politics out of elections. The passing of the Septennial Act in 1716 (requiring elections no more frequently than once every seven years) was no accident. Declining Tory morale and increasing Whig control combined to make electoral contests less necessary. No more than 190 of England's 489 seats (39 per cent) were contested at any one general election during the period 1734–1832. The general election of 1761 witnessed the nadir of English political quiescence when only four English counties and 40 boroughs polled. Among smaller English and Welsh boroughs – defined as those with electorates of fewer than 500 – only 18 contests were held in that year. Thereafter, there was something of a revival and several of the late eighteenth- and early nineteenth-century general elections were comparatively keenly contested. In the larger boroughs, the number of contests increased sharply from the 1770s on. Nevertheless, no general election in the half-century before the Reform Act saw more than 11 county contests or more than 82 borough ones.

It would be easy to conclude from the foregoing survey that the old electoral system was not only unrepresentative but also supine, slothful and corrupt, giving the Whig oligarchs of Hanoverian England licence to do as they liked when they liked. Were things as awful as they seemed? The researches of Professors O'Gorman and Phillips during the last 15 years give a rather different picture (4, 5, 6). Historians have too readily latched on to the excesses of the old system and have either ignored, or considerably downplayed, its ability both to represent a diversity of interests and to engender change. Professor O'Gorman argues that historians have been far too prone to generalize from 'anecdotes and examples – usually of a singular character – . . . to demonstrate how electors behaved'. All too easily is a picture built up of what O'Gorman ironically calls 'the dark age before 1832' (4, p. 4). It is worth a fresh look both at who the pre-1832 voters were and also at how their interests were represented.

One problem has been the tendency to excessive polarization about the old system. It has long been recognized that the old system *did* accommodate diversity. However, the general conclusion has been that in a small number of boroughs (about 20 in all) very large electorates ensured real choice and very limited landowner influence. In these places, furthermore, voters from most ranks in society were encountered. Elsewhere, it has been assumed, great landowners with sufficiently large reserves of cash – and many of them were exceedingly wealthy – needed to consult no other interests than their own as they bribed and manipulated an electorate largely of property owners who either shared their own prejudices or could be readily induced to do so.

In the largest boroughs, naturally enough, many of the voters were relatively lowly folk. Many detailed, computer-aided, analyses of the social composition of early nineteenth-century electorates have been made in recent years and these confirm general assumptions about voters in the largest constituencies. In the general election of 1802, for example, 13 per cent of Liverpool's voters were retailers (most of them small shopkeepers), while 67 per cent were craftsmen, mostly apprenticed

11

workers in steady employment but – to use a slightly anachronistic term – distinctly 'working class'. Even in more socially eligible Chester between 1812 and 1826, only 14 per cent of voters were gentlemen, professionals or manufacturers, while 80 per cent were retailers or craftsmen.

The interesting conclusion to emerge from the detailed analyses of O'Gorman and Phillips, however, is that many voters of relatively humble social origin are found in the smaller boroughs also. An analysis of 32 borough constituencies of varying size discovered that only 14 per cent of electors were gentlemen and professionals (a proportion equalled by semi-skilled and unskilled labourers, incidentally) while 60 per cent were retailers and craftsmen. It seems a fair conclusion that the electorates of pre-reform England were dominated by what might be termed the lower-middle and the upper-working classes. Not only must simple images of privileged voters holding the destinies of the nation in their hands be abandoned. In terms of social representation, as we shall see, the 1832 Reform Act represented regression. As Professor Nossiter calculated in the late 1960s (admittedly from a sample of boroughs exclusively situated in the north-east of England), the category of semi- and unskilled labourers virtually disappeared from the electoral map after 1832, while retailers and craftsmen also shrank as a proportion, albeit marginally. Professor O'Gorman's conclusion is inescapable: 'The unreformed electorate . . . reached quite far down the social scale, beneath the artisanate and into the labouring classes to an extent that the Great Reform Act could not emulate . . . the structure of the electorate was not . . . a bad representation of the social structure in general' (4, p. 216).

It is, of course, perfectly consistent to discover a socially representative electorate which is nevertheless bribed, threatened and otherwise forced to the polls in support of candidates selected by a member of the aristocracy. Relatively poor voters might be thought to appreciate a bribe, or limitless supplies of free drink during the poll, at least as much as their social superiors. But was the eighteenth-century electorate as corrupt as it has been painted? Perhaps even more important, was such corruption as there was used to drive through a landowner's will or was it, perhaps, part of a much subtler process of accommodation and mutual interest? Eighteenth-century Britain, it is clear, was ruled by great landowners, but did those landowners consider only their own desires? Did they anyway always get what they wanted?

Recent research gives diverse answers. While recognizing that great landowners *influenced* a substantial majority of parliamentary seats before 1832, it suggests that they actually *controlled* far fewer. The most recent calculations suggest that by the beginning of the nineteenth century only about 180 MPs were directly nominated by a borough patron and a substantial minority of these were Scottish members. In Scotland, electoral vitality was considerably less than in England. Perhaps 70 or 80 seats were so large that they were beyond any realistic or systematic influence. This meant that a majority of seats, while under electoral influence, were by no means permanently safe. In such seats, landowners, or the government – before 1832 the biggest 'patron' of all – needed to consult electors and hopes of success frequently required far more than the siphoning of large quantities of liquor down receptive voters' gullets.

The consequences of this arithmetic are extremely important for our understanding of the nature of the unreformed electorate. In many county and larger borough seats patrons and candidates needed to involve themselves in what Professor O'Gorman calls 'a complex and long-term dialogue with the community, its social and economic requirements, and its leaders and their personal and familial interests' (4, p. 386). In such constituencies, particularly as divisive political and religious issues became more prominent in the wake of the American and French Revolutions in the last quarter of the eighteenth century, electors became more politically conscious. What might be called the 'Hogarthian' image of an election was increasingly being challenged by a new one which reflected debate, dialogue and even demand from an aware electorate. This does not mean that landowners were regularly taken on and beaten by the unreformed electorate. Increasingly, however, landowners became highly aware of those political, religious, social or economic issues which mattered to the communities whose political allegiance they sought. Elections might even have operated both as a safety valve for alienating discontent and as a conduit (however long and tortuous) for eventual political change. Certainly, voter opinion mattered in a large number of parliamentary constituencies, where it increasingly reflected wider public opinion.

The pendulum must not be allowed to swing too far. To read some pages of Professors O'Gorman and Phillips, one can almost be forgiven for wondering why any significant head of steam should ever have built up for a change in such a reciprocal and beneficial political system. It cannot be denied that the old system sustained huge flaws and anomalies. By the 1780s these were being brought with increasing frequency to the attention of parliament. Yet before moving on to consider why reform became such a central issue, we should acknowledge that the workings of the pre-reformed electoral system were complex and subtle. Perhaps the phrase 'participatory oligarchy' might be coined to describe how it worked. The phrase acknowledges that voters, and even non-voting members of larger boroughs, had more of a forum for expression of opinion, and frequently exerted much greater political influence at grass-roots level, than is generally acknowledged.

3
Why did pressure for parliamentary reform grow?

Criticism of the unreformed system grew markedly in the second half of the eighteenth century. Those who desired change fell into two categories. First, there were those, mainly from the propertied classes with access to influential friends if not influential themselves, who wished to eliminate the worst features of the old system, but they envisaged control of government remaining firmly in the hands of men of property and education. Few of these reformers would countenance anything approaching 'one man, one vote'. Many were dissenters from the Church of England. Dissenters had increased markedly in numbers since the Glorious Revolution of 1688, after which they could worship freely but could not, at least in theory, hold any local or central government office. Nor could they attend either of the English universities, Oxford or Cambridge. A consistent strain of reformist opinion during the eighteenth century was dissenter. For much of the century, campaigns to remove civil disabilities from dissenters took priority over agitation to reform parliament.

The second reformist category comprised those, mostly without much property, who saw participation in the choosing of a nation's rulers as an essential right of all its citizens, regardless of wealth. Sadly, few would have categorized women as citizens. For all but a very tiny minority the demand for 'universal male adult suffrage' meant precisely that.

The parliamentary reform movement grew for three main reasons. Within parliament and, more especially among voters in county constituencies, disquiet was growing at the way in which influence or patronage determined matters at Westminster. It seemed particularly objectionable that an ineffective and unpopular government could keep itself in office by putting pressure on those members representing rotten boroughs controlled by government supporters (including the crown) to vote solidly for it. Lord North's ministry (1770–82) was prolonged at least three years by George III's determination to uphold it by the exercise of royal patronage, even against the judgement of a prime minister who was anxious to quit. Many country gentlemen thought it monstrous that a government responsible for the disasters of the American War of Independence and the loss of the American colonies should thus be kept in office. Their representatives in the Commons, the English county MPs, normally supported the government of the day, but after 1777, when the battle of Saratoga was lost, they began to desert it. Yet North survived even this. The numerical under-representation of the county MPs was forcibly impressed upon them, which was the more galling since county members were in general the most independent-minded and least corruptible in the House.

Not surprisingly, one of the earliest reform movements, that founded in Yorkshire in 1779 by the Revd Christopher Wyvill, called for increased county representation and for various checks on the government, the most notable of which was the need to fight elections more frequently. Its members, overwhelmingly, were landowners – Wyvill himself was a landowning Anglican clergyman – and its target the corruption of the executive. William Pitt the Younger introduced two reform bills, one as a backbencher and one as prime minister. Both augmented Wyvill's theme by attempting to increase the number of 'uncorrupted boroughs'. In May 1783, a proposal to increase the number of county and large borough seats received 149 votes in the Commons but was defeated by more than 150 votes. Pitt's enhanced prestige as prime minister in 1785 increased his parliamentary support to 174 votes but his proposal to compensate the owners of 36 rotten boroughs for their loss of property and transfer their seats to the counties and to London was still defeated by more than 70 votes.

The second spur to parliamentary reform was economic

change. The under-representation of Britain's leading commercial and industrial centres (see pp. 5–7) became the more difficult to justify with every year that passed. Some unofficial arrangements had been made. After 1774, Birmingham manufacturers exercised influence in the nomination for one of Warwickshire's county seats and this partially compensated for the lack of direct representation for the town before 1832. The business community of Southwark, in south London, secured the return of a radical MP, Sir Joseph Mawbey, for one of the two Surrey county seats in 1770, much to the disgust of many country gentlemen. Economic changes significantly affected the social composition of many county electorates. If a town was not a parliamentary borough, then its inhabitants qualified for a county vote on the normal freehold qualification. Urban prosperity created many such 'town' voters in county seats, not all of them in the more obvious industrial areas. In the two decades before the Reform Act, for example, urban-based voters represented a third or more of all electors in Cambridgeshire, Durham, Hampshire, Kent and Surrey. Counties with more obvious industrial development at this time, notably Yorkshire and Warwickshire, had only a fifth or so.

In these circumstances, it is hardly surprising that some country squires felt that their influence in rural England was beginning to be diluted by urban interests. Most of rural England, it is true, remained instinctively anti-reformist, but some could see the merit of creating more genuinely urban seats in order to confirm and permanently sustain the domination of the agricultural interest in county seats. It is not at all surprising that a parliament of landowners, in biting the reform bullet, seized the opportunity to nourish the interest of the counties. Thus, while Birmingham, Manchester, Sheffield and the rest obtained their separate representation in 1832, the number of English county seats was increased by 80 per cent (from 80 to 144; see Appendix 3). In many of these county seats, furthermore, the urban influence was substantially reduced.

The third reason was ideological and, ultimately, the most powerful. In the second half of the eighteenth century European writers and philosophers, particularly in France, were redefining the relationship between the individual and the state. This was one aspect of the so-called European Enlightenment. Most of its advocates believed that the authority of governments over their

17

subjects ultimately rested upon an implicit contract between governors and governed, whereby the governed gave up certain rights of independent action and initiative to the governors in return for benefits which only a government could bestow, such as security and a framework of laws to protect society from internal and external enemies. From this line of reasoning, it followed that ordinary men possessed basic rights which no government could take away. Jean-Jacques Rousseau's book, *Du Contrat Social*, published in 1762, argued that any contract between governors and governed rested on the right of each citizen to participate in the choosing of his governors. Democracy, therefore, was the only legitimate basis for the exercise of authority by any government. The ideas of Rousseau and other Enlightenment thinkers directly challenged the despots who ruled most European states, but they also came to have a profound impact in Britain, which was certainly not an autocracy, but which was equally far from being a democracy. Britain was a type of oligarchy since power was exercised by a subtle blend of monarchy with limited, but not negligible, powers and a parliament controlled by wealthy landowners.

For those who sympathized with the Enlightenment, Britain's hybrid government was scarcely less objectionable than a despotism. When the French Revolution broke out in 1789 it was seen as a supreme vindication of the new thinking and the parliamentary reform movement gained immensely by its example. After 1789, British writers and intellectuals from the middle ranks of society had much more success in carrying their message down the social scale, at least as far as the skilled working men in cities like London, Sheffield and Norwich which had a high proportion of craftsmen who were both literate and politically aware. The book which became the bible of such men, Tom Paine's *The Rights of Man*, appeared in two parts in 1791–2; it rapidly became one of the eighteenth century's bestsellers. It stated universal manhood suffrage to be the only legitimate basis for government; it anticipated and even prophesied the imminent collapse of all European monarchies, including the British; it advocated disarmament, since democracies would never need to make war on one another; it proposed swingeing, confiscatory taxes on all inherited wealth, a hereditary landowner appearing to Paine as an absurd concept. With the money saved on defence and collected in taxes,

Tom Paine's democracy would establish free, compulsory education, pensions, family allowances and a range of welfare benefits most of which were not to be widely available in Britain until after 1945.

Paine's work owed everything to the European Enlightenment. It was a work of supreme propaganda, simplifying complex or abstract concepts in language which a wider audience could readily understand; it was racily written and well spiced with telling epigrams. 'Aristocracy', Paine gleefully told his readers, 'has a tendency to degenerate the human species.' Inheritance laws produced grotesque anomalies. A hereditary monarch, he argued, was as absurd a concept as a hereditary mathematician. 'It requires some talent to be a common mechanic; but to be a king requires only the animal figure of a man – a sort of breathing automaton.' Nor should the wisdom of past ages serve as any guide to government in the future: 'The vanity and presumption of governing beyond the grave is the most ridiculous and insolent of all tyrannies.' Political rights were not to be willed away on the corrupt 'manuscript authority of the dead'.

It is not difficult to see how such language might appeal directly to an audience of skilled working people anxious for advancement and susceptible to the cruel over-simplification that all hardships derived from the illegitimate exercise of power by government. Even when they fell into poverty, Paine had a word for their predicament. The poor laws were imposed by unfeeling authority and operated as 'instruments of civil torture'. Legitimate power, artisans learned from Paine, could only be given by the governed. In the 1790s, the overwhelming majority of the governed had no opportunity to bestow it in a free election.

The French Revolution was a watershed in the history of parliamentary reform. Before it, pressure came primarily from the middle and even the upper ranks. After 1789, though these groups were by no means eclipsed, the reform movement was increasingly influenced by democrats who sought a government with a much broader social base, and regularly elected by universal male suffrage. As the industrial revolution concentrated ever more people in the towns of south-east Lancashire, the West Riding of Yorkshire and the central valley of Scotland, so the arguments for such a government grew. How could a parliament of landowners, representing places like Dunwich or West Looe, possibly know how to govern cotton spinners from Bolton or weavers from Paisley?

4

Parliamentary reformers, 1789–1820

The campaign to secure a reform of parliament pre-dated the French Revolution. The activities of parliamentary reformers before 1789 have been well covered by Professors Rudé, Christie and Cannon (1, 8, 9). Working men were frequently involved in radical movements. London craftsmen associated with the complex and demagogic intrigues of John Wilkes in the 1760s and early 1770s were only one group. Established commercial centres such as Norwich and Birmingham were also centres of opposition to a landed, Anglican oligarchy. However, the activities of parliamentary reformers before 1789 were dominated by . the urban middle classes and by country gentlemen. Both groups feared the extension of government (executive) control over the parliamentary legislature by means of influence and corruption and they found an effective voice as they hounded Lord North in the last five years of his administration (see chapter 3 above). Reform was advocated as a cleansing and purifying agent. Reformers were strongest in London, where the leading pressure group was the Society for Constitutional Information (SCI), and in Yorkshire, England's largest county and one which always carefully burnished its reputation for independence of thought. However, once the Younger Pitt had established himself as prime minister, and especially after the general election of 1784 secured the position of a premier who had played on somewhat tenuous credentials as a reformer, their cause waned.

Undoubtedly, the French Revolution of 1789 revived the reform cause generally and focused it increasingly upon the reform of parliament. The overthrow of Europe's most powerful autocracy and its replacement by a National Assembly allegedly favouring those noble, if amorphous, ideals of liberty, equality and fraternity inspired reformers everywhere. In Britain the chairman of the Society for Constitutional Information, the MP Henry Flood, raised the reform issue in the Commons in March 1790. Avoiding the impression that he was a wild revolutionary, he advocated a widening of the franchise to include house-holders, but stopped well short of universal male suffrage. 'Numbers', he dutifully told the House, 'are necessary to the spirit of liberty.' But he recognized that property must continue to exercise the decisive influence because property was 'conducive to the spirit of order'. He also indicated that he favoured reform precisely because he was 'no friend to revolutions . . . I am, therefore, a friend to timely reform, and for this reason, that it renders revolutions unnecessary'.

Flood's motion did not reach a vote, but his speech is important in indicating a line of reasoning much favoured by middle-class and aristocratic reformers right up to 1832. Most wished to preserve a government rooted in property rather than 'mere numbers'; not to reform, however, would be the most dangerous course of all. Men without hope of change or concession from their governors would look to bloody revolution. Particularly once the French Revolution moved into its 'terror' phase from 1792, with Jacobins in control, the French king and queen executed and what appeared to alarmed observers in Britain to be a wholesale march of the aristocracy to the guillotine, the argument of 'reform in order to preserve' gained strength. Even so, the majority view in parliament remained that the best way to guard against revolution in Britain was to stamp early and firmly on any manifestation of support for 'French principles'.

Outside parliament, the SCI produced large numbers of pamphlets in favour of reform, many of them advocating democracy. By May 1792 the society was even sending letters of encouragement to the Jacobin club in Paris, assuring it of steadily increasing support in Britain. John Horne Tooke, an active radical since the 1760s, and other SCI leaders were making contact with working men, educating them in political organization and urging them to establish their own societies. The results were spectacular. A Constitutional Society was founded in Sheffield late in 1791 and over the next two years a string of radical societies of working men were founded in most of Britain's larger towns. Especially prominent were the established craft and trade centres, such as Norwich, Newcastle, Perth and Edinburgh. Large numbers of literate skilled workers lived in these towns and for them the message of political advancement through organization, correspondence and education was particularly attractive. Central Scotland, indeed, was the main focus of radical activity in 1792–3. In Perth, for example, a symbolic 'Tree of Liberty' was planted and a report from November 1792 argued that 'The lower class of people talk of nothing but liberty and equality' (**12**, p. 70).

Most of the new societies in England took both their name and their lead from the London Corresponding Society (LCS), founded in January 1792 by a Scottish shoemaker, Thomas Hardy, with active assistance from Tooke. As the names of these societies indicate, they spread reform doctrines throughout the country by correspondence and other expressions of mutual support. Meetings were held in local public houses; constitutions of extraordinary precision were drawn up; tracts and pamphlets were published; the French were bombarded with messages of support. Their intellectual inspiration was Tom Paine (see pp. 18–19) and their commitment to one man, one vote followed the arguments in *The Rights of Man*. Corresponding society members bought huge numbers of copies of the cheap editions of a book whose arguments formed the basis of many a public house discussion.

In fostering working men's political societies, was the SCI nursing a viper at its bosom? On one interpretation, the mobilization of working-class support was necessary to mount the kind of pressure for reform which the government could not ignore. But after 1792 parliamentary reform would never again be dominated by polite discussion among articulate intellectuals, lawyers and radical manufacturers and entrepreneurs influenced by enlightenment thinking. In the 1790s artisans were not as a group so vulnerable to unemployment and grinding poverty as were the growing number of unapprenticed and less skilled labourers. However, the economic dimension was never far from their thinking. A substantial proportion of the support for reform which built up in the years 1792–5 was strongly influenced by economic considerations. Radical working men looked to political reform as a buttress against rising prices and unemployment. Few workers could afford the luxury of dispassionate appeals to reason. For them, democracy offered a more potent weapon in the struggle for improvement and independence.

Not all of this was clear to those members of the SCI, and there were many, who distrusted democracy. Horne Tooke was a case in point: he was a radical and a libertarian, but no democrat. He assisted working-class radical societies in 1791 and 1792 because he believed in their power to strengthen the pressure for reform, but he could hardly applaud when they hastened to pass resolutions in favour of universal manhood suffrage and the abolition of both monarchy and the House of Lords. Nor, as a beneficed clergyman, did he approve the tendency in many societies towards free-thought and atheism. He had helped to unleash a force which he could not control.

At the beginning of their brief career, the corresponding societies had believed that their objectives could be achieved by organization and the petitioning of parliament. In this delusion they were encouraged partly by the writings of Paine, which conveyed the naive impression that issues were decided on the basis of strength of argument, and partly by a new organization of aristocratic Whig politicans, the Association of the Friends of the People, founded in April 1792. This exclusive club, with the prohibitively high annual subscription of 2½ guineas, attracted young reformers like Charles Grey, Thomas Erskine and William Lambton as well as some older ones such as Viscount Lauderdale and the established playwright R. B. Sheridan. Its members were contemptuous of the fears of Whigs further to the right, who were now rapidly turning against reform, but they were also anxious to control the direction of radical agitation. Most of them feared democracy as much as the most fervent anti-reformers, but they calculated that the best way of avoiding it was to 'adopt' the radical societies and channel their enthusiasms in a safe direction. For a time, they succeeded. The Friends of the People helped to orchestrate a petitioning campaign which led to a debate in the Commons on the principle of reform in May 1793. Grey, in proposing the motion, was at pains to clarify that its supporters rejected ideas from France:

'it was impossible that any set of men, who had not actually lost their senses, should ever propose the French revolution as a model for imitation'. The case for reform was, as reformist Whigs would continue to assert down to 1832, that change was necessary in order to preserve the essentials of the constitution. His argument was based 'not on natural right, but upon what was in itself the best system of government, and most conducive to the happiness of the country'. Too many people now felt excluded from a government structure which, he alleged, had actually increased the power of the crown (a reliable stand-by of all Whigs in opposition throughout the eighteenth century) and of the House of Lords. Change would therefore conserve, not subvert, the essentials of government by the best.

Grey knew that his motion stood no chance of success. Indeed, he had begun to doubt the wisdom of carrying on with it at all. Since the Friends had conceived the idea of a debate backed by petitions for reform, Louis XVI had been executed by the revolutionaries. The following month – February 1793 – Britain declared war on revolutionary France. By May, parliamentary opinion had never been so hostile to reform. Grey's motion was lost by 282 votes to 41. Grey confessed himself to a friend 'in despair', not so much that he had lost but that the consequence of defeat would see a people 'maddened by excessive injury and roused to a feeling of their own strength [not stopping] within the limits of moderation'.

Extra-parliamentary reformers now struggled in an intensely unfavourable climate. Scottish reformers, encouraged by two conventions in 1792 and early 1793, invited the English radical societies to send representatives to a national convention in Edinburgh in November and December 1793. The very title, taken directly from France, alarmed the authorities. Some radicals were indeed toying with the idea of declaring that they, rather than an unrepresentative parliament, were the true leaders of the people, since parliament had so contemptuously rejected their petitions. The authorities now felt ready to move, and the London Corresponding Society delegates, Maurice Margarot and Joseph Gerrald, were arrested together with the Scottish secretary of the convention, William Skirving, charged with sedition, and sentenced to transportation for fourteen years (**14, 11**).

Increasingly secure of the support of propertied opinion, the government now mounted a direct attack on the radicals. The suspension of Habeas Corpus in May 1794 enabled political suspects to be held indefinitely without trial. A dozen leading reformers from the SCI and the LCS were arrested on charges of treason, and although a London jury refused to convict the three, including Hardy and Tooke, who were eventually brought to trial, the episode frightened many reformers. Neither Hardy nor Tooke played a significant role in radical leadership again; Tooke even allowed himself to be selected for parliament in 1801 for the rotten borough of Old Sarum under the patronage of the Earl of Caledon. Once the government had bared its teeth, propertied reformers from the Friends of the People and the SCI showed every sign of fearing the bite. They also responded in some measure to patriotic rallying cries during the war. Though both groups helped the corresponding societies to mount impressive public demonstrations against the Seditious Meetings and Treasonable Practices Acts which the government rushed through parliament during the economic depression at the end of 1795 and which significantly curtailed both meetings and political debate, the government's policy against the radicals succeeded almost totally. The LCS, which had a membership of 5,000 at its peak and at least as many active sympathizers, became after 1795 a small, isolated group, deprived of its normal channels of communication by the 'Two Acts' and dominated in its final years by revolutionaries seeking an alliance with Irish republicans and the French to bring the government down by force. Its last public meeting, in St Pancras in July 1797, was declared illegal and dispersed by the magistrates. By the time Pitt formally banned the LCS in 1799 it had totally lost its old power to bring crowds onto the streets and it had almost no middle-class allies.

Grey, meanwhile, made a final effort. In May 1797, he dusted down a plan drawn up by the Whig Friends of the People in 1795 and presented it to the Commons. The proposal was for a straight householder franchise in the boroughs, together with an increased electorate in the counties. Each constituency would return one member, rather than two. He deliberately chose a time of maximum difficulty for the government. The war was going badly; economic discontent was manifest and the government was forced to raise taxes. Grey hoped for independent support, such as had been available to the opposition in 1780–2 when Lord North had finally been toppled. The circumstances of 1797, however, were entirely different. The Younger Pitt was no North and had every intention of carrying on. Fear of France, perhaps even of a successful French invasion, was paramount. Although Grey mustered the largest vote of any opposition motion since the war had begun, he still lost decisively, by 256 votes to 91.

From 1797 to 1815, when the French wars finally ended, the reform question was generally in the background, but the period is not without importance. High food prices and widespread unemployment brought pro-reform crowds on to the streets of the new Lancashire cotton towns in 1797 and 1801. A growing political awareness in the industrial areas was to be an important factor in the later phases of the reform campaign. At the general election of 1802 reformers could take at least two crumbs of comfort from results in the larger constituencies: Sir Francis Burdett, a wealthy radical, was elected at Middlesex while in Norwich the arch anti-reformer, William Windham, was defeated by a nonconformist reformer, William Smith.

The reformers' main problem in keeping the pot boiling was the lukewarmness of the Whig opposition. Reformers were a minority in the Whig party and when Samuel Whitbread, one of their leaders, began attending reform meetings in London in 1809 he was bitterly criticized by his colleagues, including Grey whose passions had notably cooled since 1797. In their turn the radicals poured scorn on a venture sponsored by the Whigs which did achieve success. In 1809 the Whig MP John Christian Curwen got a Bribery Act onto the statute book. It prescribed fines and disqualification for any member of parliament who offered inducements to vote. But no one tried hard to make the Act work and bribery continued as before. Burdett's proposal to enfranchise householders was overwhelmingly defeated in the same year and in 1810 a better prepared case by Thomas Brand for a similar franchise extension and the reduction of parliament's maximum life to three years was defeated by 234 to 115. Brand's motion represented progress. No reform proposal had received more than 100 votes in the Commons since Pitt's in 1785.

The renewed impetus for reform, however, came from outside parliament. In the last years of the war economic warfare between Britain and France almost stifled Britain's overseas markets, resulting in widespread unemployment and rocketing food prices. The consequent distress offered fertile soil for the radical message of reformers such as Major John Cartwright who made a tour of the Midlands and northern industrial areas to spread the gospel of reform based on collaboration between the middle and working classes. In 1812 a group of prosperous London-based radicals, led by Cartwright and Burdett (now MP for Westminster) had formed a Hampden club, named after one of the foremost opponents of Charles I's personal rule in the 1630s, to agitate for a franchise of taxpayers.

Cartwright succeeded in stimulating reform activity in the north, but the results were not what he anticipated. Peace returned in 1815 accompanied by further economic distress and the main manufacturing areas began to organize radical movements of their own. These showed a healthy aversion to following the lead of middle-class and aristocratic reform associations. The provincial Hampden Clubs, particularly numerous in the weaving villages of south Lancashire, called for full manhood suffrage and they organized a massive petitioning campaign in 1816–17. The 1817 parliamentary session received over 700 petitions from 350 towns, mostly from the manufacturing areas of the Midlands, Lancashire, Yorkshire and central Scotland. The London radicals also arranged huge political meetings at which the tub-thumping oratory of yet another middle-class reformer, Henry ('Orator') Hunt, made a great impression.

The revival of reform between 1812 and 1817 is noteworthy in several respects: it was on a much broader scale than anything seen before, but, more significantly, it was no longer directed from London. Though the capital remained important, the focus of attention had shifted northwards to precisely those areas where political representation was most flimsy and where the growth of population and manufacturing industry most suggested the need for change. The growth of political awareness in both large factories and small workshops was most marked. The circulation of radical newspapers, led by the weekly *Cobbett's Political Register* but ably and wittily supported by Thomas Wooler's *Black Dwarf* and William Sherwin's *Political Register*, was unprecedentedly large. By 1820 government publications were outnumbered, out-written and out-argued by pro-reform material.

A crucial theme of this propaganda after 1815 was that the target was not only an unrepresentative, but a corrupt, government. The belief, harboured by many radical artisans and other workers in the period 1789–1832, that political reform offered a route to economic improvement was not so illogical as it seemed. Cobbett was the best-known radical journalist, and perhaps the more effective for having been a Tory supporter until the early years of the nineteenth century and thus intimately acquainted with both the strengths and the weaknesses of the anti-reform position. When asked how an adjustment to parliamentary constituencies and an increase in the number of voters could possibly provide material help to workers at, or below, the bread-line, he had his answer ready. Corrupt governments spent taxpayers' hard-earned money on themselves, not on the nation. So, to eliminate corruption would be to provide material benefit for working people. His famous *Political Register* trumpeted in December 1816:

> As to the causes of our present miseries, it is the *enormous amount of the taxes*, which the government compels us to pay for the support of its army, its placemen, its pensioners etc., and for the payment of the interest of its debt. . . . The *remedy* is what we have now to look to, and that remedy consists wholly and solely of such a *reform* of the Commons or People's House of Parliament, as shall give to every payer of *direct taxes* a vote at elections, and as shall cause the Members to be *elected annually*.

The attack on corruption, furthermore, was one upon which both workers and the middle classes could combine. After 1815, more concerted attacks upon an aristocratic parliament *as such* were mounted by those largely or wholly excluded from representation there. In the right circumstances, workers and manufacturers could find a common platform from which to launch potent assaults by the 'productive' against what they called the 'unproductive' classes. On this line of argument, while both workers and manufacturers laboured mightily to increase the nation's wealth, inherited property owners reduced if not entirely wasted it.

If this alliance was never one of equals, it is nevertheless clear that working men were now better able to argue their own case and no longer needed the teacher–pupil relationship which had existed between the SCI and the LCS in 1792. The manufacturers' political awareness had been much sharpened by the economic confusion, privation and loss of markets which accompanied the last years of the French wars. The focus of the new concerted attacks, however, was a new Corn Law, which parliament passed in 1815. This restricted the import of foreign corn into Britain; its primary purpose was to keep domestic prices high in the interests of farmers and landowners. It was denounced as 'class' legislation, and manufacturers argued that landowners were feathering their own nests. Not only were industrialists denied similar protective legislation, but, since the Corn Law kept food prices high, it was reducing the amount of cash available for workers to buy manufactured goods. Working men argued that protection for those whose interests were fully represented in parliament meant crippling prices for the basic necessity of life for the rest of the community. The new Corn Law provided perfect ammunition to attack the unreformed political system.

The reform agitation of 1815–20 took several forms. In addition to a ceaseless propaganda blast in the reform press, an attempted armed march by weavers from Manchester to London in 1817 was broken up by the yeomanry at Stockport. This was called the 'March of the Blanketeers' from the covering which the demonstrators took with them on their projected long journey. An actual rebellion in Derbyshire (the Pentridge Rising) the same year was foiled and its leaders executed. In the summer of 1819, during a severe trade recession, four massive political rallies were held in large cities. At the last of these, in St Peter's Fields, Manchester, in August, the local yeomanry forcibly dispersed the crowds by a sabre charge, killing eleven people in the process. These victims of the 'Peterloo Massacre' (a name coined in ironic reference to the Battle of Waterloo) became the most celebrated martyrs in the cause of parliamentary reform. Peterloo 'nationalized' the reformist temper as nothing before. In the north-east and in Staffordshire, for example, where support had previously not been strong, new reform unions were established. The government felt obliged to respond, as Pitt's had done in 1794–5, with new repressive legislation. The 'Six Acts' of December 1819 prohibited arming and drilling, gave magistrates new powers to control public meetings and imposed heavy new taxes on the press in an attempt to stem the flood of anti-government propaganda.

Probably the Cato Street conspiracy of 1820 – a botched and

government-infiltrated attempt to blow up the Cabinet and take power by *coup d'état* – strengthened the government. There were always far more reformers than there were supporters of revolution. Many who wanted to see a wider and more representative electorate felt that the hanging of Arthur Thistlewood and his fellow conspirators was entirely appropriate punishment. Nevertheless, the sustained radical pressure of the period 1815–20 left a permanent mark. In the general elections of both 1818 and 1820, more radical candidates than usual contested seats. Lord Egremont, whose power base was in still largely rural Sussex, declared after the second of these that 'the Radicals & Revolutionaries are powerful and rising everywhere, & I very much fear that dangerous times are at hand' (4, p. 308). It was clear that, although the return of prosperity might push reform further down the political agenda for much of the 1820s, it could no longer remove it. Parliamentary reform was becoming a question not of 'whether' but of 'when'.

5
Why were the earlier reformers unsuccessful?

Given the amount of radical agitation in the two generations before the Reform Act, it seems sensible to ask why parliamentary reform was delayed until 1832. Ironically the very event which gave reformers most encouragement, the French Revolution, also made the passage of a reform bill through parliament much less likely.

This irony is easily unravelled. Before 1789, reform was a respectable topic for polite debate. Few disagreed that the old system was capricious and haphazard, or denied that the rise of new economic forces strengthened the case for constitutional change. Few wished to see Manchester or Birmingham permanently without direct representatives. Yet equally few in parliament would accept a reform which changed the very nature of the British constitution. Thus when changes were discussed, they were envisaged as growing naturally out of a system whose glory (so its defenders asserted) was its flexibility and diversity (see p. 52).

The change which came about after 1789 was precisely the change in established opinion which converted Pitt the Younger from a reformer to a firm political conservative. The French Revolution had inspired the politically unrepresented throughout Western Europe but it thoroughly alarmed a generation of aristocrats. Reformers became tarred with the undiscriminating brush of revolution and any attempt to disturb Britain's precisely poised constitution could be interpreted as pushing it towards the wildest of Jacobin excesses. As early as 1790, during Flood's reform motion (see p. 22), William Windham was making a point which would be flung incessantly at that dwindling band of MPs who favoured change: 'Would he [Flood] recommend you to repair your house in the hurricane season?' Virtually the whole of Pitt's speech against Grey's reform proposals in 1793 was a tirade against the 'excesses and outrages' associated with 'French principles'. All reformers were guilty by association. Pitt, as an old reformer, was careful to absolve himself. He would, he said, 'rather forgo for ever the advantages of reform, than risk for a moment the existence of the British constitution'.

The widening of the reformers' social base further weakened their attractiveness in Parliament. What the reformers *were* was at least as important as what they said. The artisans and other working men of the corresponding societies in the 1790s bore an unacceptable resemblance to the Jacobin *sans-culottes* and petty traders of Paris. Even had this parallel not been available, it is unlikely that a parliament of educated, privileged men would willingly have conceded the kind of franchise reforms which would see members elected by men who were so much their social inferiors. The existing political system might be irrational, but it did guarantee a legislature dominated by men of property, education and pedigree; to these men universal manhood suffrage was a recipe for ignorance and chaos. Men like Sheridan and Grey who advocated the kind of reforms which Pitt and many others still in parliament had supported ten years earlier were now dismissed as dupes. In the revolution which would follow reform, Pitt argued, democrats would push propertied reformers aside just as surely as they pushed the anti-reformers.

Had the French Revolution not intervened, it is most likely that a modest measure of parliamentary reform, certainly including an extension of county and large-borough representation and probably also some rationalization of the voting qualification, would have been passed in the 1790s, and William Pitt the Younger might well have been its sponsor. The Revolution also cast a long shadow. Not only were reform prospects blighted in the 1790s but memories of 1789 were to counsel caution in the next generation. Pitt died in 1806, but those who had come to prominence under him – Liverpool, Castlereagh and Canning – remained hostile to reform into the 1820s for much the same reasons as Pitt himself. It is worth noting that all three of these acolytes of William Pitt were born within months of each other in 1769 and 1770. They were therefore in their early twenties when the French Revolution moved into its terror phase. The impact remained with them throughout their political careers.

The case of Canning is particularly instructive. He is known to students primarily for his 'liberal' foreign policy, for fostering nations in South America struggling to break free from the old Spanish and Portuguese colonial empires. He also strongly supported removing political disabilities from Roman Catholics. He was not by any stretch of the imagination a general opponent of change. Yet on the question of parliamentary reform he never wavered. He had first come to prominence in 1797 as editor of the *Anti-Jacobin*, a periodical produced to stiffen the resolve of the propertied classes against the follies and dangers of reform. In another age, he might have mellowed into a moderate re-former, but the French Revolution was no ordinary political upheaval. It convinced a generation of political leaders that the fight against parliamentary reform was a crusade for civilization.

Reaction to the French Revolution, therefore, made many politicians totally hostile to parliamentary reform. The re-formed Tory party, as we may call the anti-reform coalition fashioned by Pitt and the erstwhile Whig Duke of Portland in 1794, acted as a most powerful bastion against political change. The Pitt-Portland coalition held huge majorities in the Commons during the second half of the 1790s and retained power for most of the next 35 years. Only when the weak so-called 'Ministry of All the Talents' was in office in 1806–7 were Tories out of power before the end of 1830 (**19**).

Perhaps also the British, or at least the English, *ancien régime* could anyway easily withstand outside pressure for change. In recent years, Dr Jonathan Clark has produced a reinterpretation of eighteenth- and early nineteenth-century politics and society. It holds that support for the old system remained strong and that support for radicalism generally, and for parliamentary reform in particular, was restricted to a still small and unrepresentative elite. Historians have exaggerated its importance in an understandable, but in Clark's view anachronistic, attempt

34

to explain those rapid political shifts of the nineteenth century which would eventually lead to a parliamentary democracy. He asserts that, as late as the election of 1818, 'Parliamentary reform as such remained an abstract question of principle which manifestly failed to evoke a mass response' (7, p. 371). On this line of reasoning, of course, there is nothing to explain and historians should rather direct their attention to why the old system did eventually collapse so suddenly in 1832. Clark argues that, despite the massive population growth and the increasing importance of northern and Midland industrial towns, 'there is no *objective sense* in which these things can be said to have made the electoral system inappropriate' (7, p. 36).

Clark's is a spiky, original and robustly argued view, but it has to be said that it has not commanded wide acceptance. Put simply, too many instances of change, and too many examples of politicians desperately anxious to keep the 'French contagion' out of British political life, exist for it to be credibly argued that parliamentary reform remained in the second decade of the nineteenth century the intellectual plaything of a group of nonconformist intellectuals and a few wavering Whig allies. However, we must acknowledge that some elements in Clark's 'continuity' thesis are valid. Tom Paine's optimistic prediction in 1792 that aristocratic and absolutist systems of government would all be gone from educated Europe by the turn of the century proved wildly wrong. Parliamentary reformers, when they met at their annual dinners to toast the memory of their spiritual leader (Paine died in 1809), were forced to concede that their cause would not be won swiftly or by power of argument alone.

The truth was that parliament would legislate for its own reform only under threat. The most potent threat, obviously, was fear of what might happen if parliament remained intransigent. In the 1790s, working-class support was only just beginning to be mobilized across the nation and middle-class or aristocratic reformers were easily frightened or isolated by anti-reform legislation. Sustained, concerted pressure could not be mounted on the government. Between 1812 and 1820 the reformers' strength outside parliament grew enormously. The alliance between the middle and working classes, however, (pp. 28–31), was still too new and too fragile to frighten parliament into submission and it was all too likely to be disturbed by conflict between manufacturer and workforce over rates of pay or conditions of work. In parliament, determination to resist reform remained strong while memories of the French Revolution remained fresh. Radical Whigs, like Brougham, Burdett or Romilly, had the greatest difficulty in persuading their leadership that reform was a worthwhile cause for an opposition to espouse. Votes on reform in 1812, 1817 and 1818 show deep Whig divisions on the issue. But the changing mood of the country eventually had its effect at Westminster. By 1820 Sir Robert Peel was asking a close political colleague:

Do not you think that the tone of England . . . is more liberal . . . than the policy of the government? Public opinion never had such influence on public measures, and yet never was so dissatisfied with the share it possessed. It is growing too large for the channels it has been accustomed to run through. . . . Can we resist for seven years [the length of a parliament] reform in Parliament?

6

Retreat and revival: reform, 1820–30

Despite Peel's concern, no serious possibility of parliamentary reform existed before 1827. In 1820, the Whig leader Charles Grey was confiding to his son-in-law that he did not expect to see a Reform Act 'during my life, or even yours' (2, p. 15). For a time in 1820–1, during the farcical scandal caused by George IV's attempt to divorce his wife, Queen Caroline, the new king's irritation with his Tory ministers was such that Grey harboured almost daily expectation of a call to replace them. It never came. Even had it done so, it is most unlikely that a general parliamentary reform would have been high on the Whigs' agenda. Though the Whigs at this time are indelibly associated with parliamentary reform, it is worth remembering how deeply the question divided them. Many of those representing the most influential Whig families – men such as Devonshire, Holland, Norfolk and Carlisle – were both distrustful and fearful of extra-parliamentary radicalism and the experiences of 1815–20 had made them less, not more, inclined to press the issue.

Grey himself was ambivalent. He had in 1816 drawn up a list of four points on which the Whigs might base a policy in government. On three of them – reduced government expenditure, a more liberal foreign policy and political emancipation for Roman Catholics – he felt that party unity was likely. On the fourth, parliamentary reform, he knew that he was in for trouble. 'The experience of the last 25 years', as he confided to

Lord Fitzwilliam, had tempered his enthusiasms from the 1790s. He was 'most adverse to the sweeping and radical reforms' embraced by the Cobbetts and Hunts on public platforms up and down the land (**21**, p. 209). That sentiment remained with him at least until 1830 and for much of the intervening 30 years and more, when not prone to self-indulgent fits of gloom and threats of early retirement, 'Lord Grey of the Reform Act' in fact sought to deflect discussion away from parliamentary reform and towards what he considered more promising, and less contentious, Whig territory.

Thus in the early 1820s the Whigs were divided on reform while the Tories, secure in government once the Caroline affair blew over, were as opposed to it as ever. The return of economic prosperity reduced public agitation outside Westminster. For much of the 1820s, it was Grey's prediction, rather than Peel's, which seemed more securely grounded. Parliamentary opinion revealed much more than negligible support for moderate reform, but support which was a long way short of a majority. With no encouragement from their leader, the Whigs Lambton and Russell both introduced reform bills in 1821 and 1822. Lambton called for parliaments to be elected at least once every three years and for a householder franchise in broadly equal electoral districts. Russell, returning to ground traversed by the younger Pitt almost 40 years earlier (see Chapter 3), proposed disfranchising 100 small boroughs and transferring the seats to the largest towns and the counties. It was no coincidence that internal party calculations had revealed the smaller boroughs to be disproportionately held by government supporters! Though Russell was defeated by more than 100 votes (269 to 164), the pro-reform vote was the biggest since Pitt's in 1785. Similar bills introduced in 1823, 1824 and 1826 showed modestly reduced support, and in 1826 Russell declared that he would trouble parliament with reform no further. Perhaps more significantly, no petitions for reform were presented to parliament in the years 1824–9. During the 1826 general election, yet another which, almost as a matter of routine, confirmed Lord Liverpool's Tories in office, the question was hardly raised. Parliamentary reform seemed to be a dead duck.

What breathed life back into the question has been a subject of considerable controversy between historians. Broadly, older interpretations – perhaps subconsciously influenced by the need to explain 'progress' – stressed the inevitability of revival once economic conditions combined to increase discontent outside Westminster. Such interpretations note that reform seemed to gather ever-growing support during each depression. By 1832, reform was an idea whose time had come and the Whigs were merely recognizing increasingly insistent reality. A new industrial age required new constitutional arrangements, which Grey and his ministers duly provided.

Many recent opinions express dissatisfaction with such a mechanistic and 'Whiggish' view. From different perspectives, historians such as Clark, O'Gorman and Phillips (4, 6, 7) have laid much greater stress on events within Westminster. Reform could hardly have come about in 1832, they argue, had the old Tory party not been shattered by events between 1827 and 1830. There was no reason for the Whigs ever to have come into office had the Tories not imploded over religious issues. Parliamentary reform was one of the few issues on which they could agree, so the motivating force for change was, as Clark put it, 'Religion, not representation' (7, p. 388). The narrative of events at Westminster in the years 1827–30 suggests that there is much to be said for an interpretation which places emphasis on events within the old political order, rather than on clamour for change from outside it.

Liverpool's long government was ended by his stroke in February 1827. Within a year of this event, Tory politics were in total disarray. Liverpool's value to the Tories was never so apparent as in the few months after his resignation. His supreme talent lay in the ability to get naturally more gifted subordinates to work in harmony under him. Without him, the Tories squabbled and split. There were two reasons for this. The first was vanity and envy. Liverpool had a clear favourite for the succession – George Canning – but not one who would be universally acceptable to his party. A number of able and experienced men with different political perspectives and a strong sense of their own importance could consider themselves equally qualified. As always in politics, it is unwise to underestimate either the importance of vanity, rivalry and ambition in determining events or the extent to which personal hostilities (more usually seen between members of the same party than between political opponents) cloud mature judgement. The second reason, and the more 'respectable' in many historians' eyes since it stresses 'issues' rather than personality, was religion. A strong case can be made for the contention that parliamentary reform was enacted in the early 1830s because the Tories fell out over political relief for Protestant Dissenters and, particularly, Roman Catholics. An equally strong, if more cynical, one can be made for concluding that they just fell out.

After initial huffing and puffing, George IV confirmed Canning as Liverpool's successor. Canning was a brilliant man whose talent for biting sarcasm and manifest intolerance of mediocrity made him many permanent enemies. He was also distrusted among the 'Protestants' from Liverpool's Cabinet for supporting Roman Catholic emancipation (see p. 42). For men like the Duke of Wellington, Lord Eldon and Robert Peel (whose six-year period as Chief Secretary for Ireland had not softened his heart towards Catholics) the supremacy of the Anglican church was a central pillar of the established order. Allowing Catholics to sit in parliament would weaken that pillar. These three refused to serve Canning and were replaced by the Whig politicians, Tierney, Lansdowne and Carlisle, much to the annoyance of Grey and the rest of the Whig leadership. Canning's brief premiership thus split both parties. When he died after a few months he was replaced by Viscount Goderich who proved a hopelessly weak leader.

After Goderich's resignation, the Duke of Wellington was asked in January 1828 to form a government. Wellington's generally conservative views were well known and it was assumed that his term of office would greatly strengthen the anti-reformers. In fact, his ministry, which lasted almost three years, progressively demoralized them and when it fell in November 1830 it was replaced by a Whig government pledged to reform.

Early in Wellington's ministry, the Protestant Dissenters finally secured the legislative change they had been seeking for upwards of a century. In the spring of 1828, and with surprisingly little parliamentary opposition, Lord John Russell's Bill to repeal the Test and Corporation Acts was passed. Dissenters could now legally hold government office. On one level, the apparently uncontentious passage of this repeal is easily explained. The Acts had been widely circumvented and had more symbolic than practical significance in most spheres. Furthermore, the return of prosperity and evident respectability of many middle-class Dissenters persuaded many Tories not only that repeal was safe but that it might strengthen the constitution. Peel's dextrous lobbying in the House of Lords averted opposition from the bishops and without episcopal support anti-repeal Tories could not put up much of a fight. Defeat, however, rankled with some. Lord Eldon asserted that it was a 'revolutionary Bill' and recalled eminent predecessors who had considered it destructive 'of all union between Church and State'. The opposition of the 'Ultras' (as the extreme Protestant Tories soon came to be called) to their own government can be traced to what they considered a betrayal over the Test and Corporation Acts.

'Protestant' disaffection might perhaps have been finessed by a more sensitive leader than Wellington. His ineptitude as a politician needs stressing. Wellington himself would probably have denied that he was a politician at all; he expressed contempt for political squabbles and petty office-seeking. But aristocratic disdain allied to soldierly common sense were not appropriate equipment for the complex tasks which lay ahead. When events began to move rapidly, Wellington was usually behind the game. In particular, he behaved as if opposition was of no account, especially when it surfaced within his government. He had included Liberal Tories, inheritors of the Canning tradition, only reluctantly and he removed them as soon as opportunity offered. Canning's old political friends, now led by William Huskisson, had not retained his specific aversion to even modest parliamentary reform. Huskisson, Palmerston and Lamb supported the indefatigable Russell's bill to disfranchise two more corrupt small boroughs – Penryn (Cornwall) and East Retford (Nottinghamshire) – and to reallocate their seats to Manchester and Birmingham. When Peel proposed an amendment to transfer East Retford's seats instead to nearby Bassetlaw where (by no coincidence whatever) the Duke of Newcastle enjoyed unchallenged, old-style electoral influence, the Huskissonites offered to resign. To general surprise (including that of the Huskissonites themselves), Wellington accepted their offer and took the opportunity to reconstruct his government by including more anti-reformers. Though his intention may have been to hold out an olive-branch to the Ultras, the effect was to reduce the government's debating talent in the House of Commons rather than to reconcile the right to a ministry which was already proving itself unsound on religion.

A far more damaging split was precipitated by the Huskissonite departures. The president of the Board of Trade, Charles Grant, resigned with Huskisson in May 1828. His successor, William Vesey Fitzgerald, the son of an Irish peer, represented County Clare in the Commons. By a practice not finally abolished until 1926, any MP accepting government office had to resign his seat and submit himself for re-election. In normal circumstances a new minister was either returned unopposed or easily won the resulting by-election. But a movement for Catholic civil rights had been gathering momentum in Ireland during the 1820s, orchestrated by the Catholic Association, whose leader was Daniel O'Connell. O'Connell decided to oppose Fitzgerald, both as an expression of opposition to Wellington's anti-Catholic government and as a means of showing to the British the strength of Irish feelings.

O'Connell duly won a by-election rich in propaganda on both sides. The Catholics, many of whom qualified as forty-shilling freeholders though their property holdings were extremely small, voted in large numbers and the result presented the British government with an acute dilemma. O'Connell had been elected, but under existing legislation could not take his seat since he was a Catholic. If the government refused to change the law, the Catholic Association would instigate immense popular agitation. Civil unrest, including the refusal to pay rent to 'alien' English landlords or tithes to the Anglican church, was all too likely. But concessions in Ireland would be seen by Wellington's staunchest supporters as a betrayal of their most dearly held principles. Almost by choice, Wellington had got rid of the 'Liberal' Tories; he could scarcely survive a revolt by the Tory right wing. These 'Ultra-Tories' were now an important force.

When Wellington and Peel opted for peace in Ireland by granting Roman Catholic emancipation in 1829, the expected split materialized. The 'Ultras' were not appeased by the government's raising of the Irish voting qualification to £10 to exclude the dangerous Catholic peasantry. Wellington and Peel were branded traitors. The conservative alliance which had ruled Britain since the 1790s finally came to an end. Wellington, who thought himself above any squalid party battles, now found himself leading a smaller, demoralized Tory faction whose control over parliament was slipping away.

Catholic emancipation changed the complexion of parliament

utterly. George IV and Eldon, strong opponents both, complained to each other about desertion and betrayal by the government. The fact that royal opposition had patently failed to halt a measure which, in the Ultras' view, did incalculable damage to the constitution served to strengthen their impression that the old order was being undermined from within. What extra-parliamentary pressure had failed to achieve, Wellington and Peel were handing to the radicals on a plate. The consequences were bizarre. Forced, as they saw it, to make a choice between an unreformed parliament and the integrity of their beloved Church of England, many of the Ultras opted to sustain the Church. They pointed out that only government control over small boroughs had secured a majority for Catholic emancipation. The measure had little support in the country. If the people could be consulted, the argument ran, they would rally in 1829–30, as they had since the seventeenth century, to the cry of 'No popery!' Votes corruptly contrived for middle-class Irishmen by Peel and Wellington would be eagerly taken away by a parliament properly elected by free-born Englishmen. The Ultras agreed with the opinion of the newspaper *John Bull* that emancipation represented 'the complete subversion of the principles upon which our Constitution has been founded'.

Thus it was that the first proposals for parliamentary reform during a crisis which culminated in the passage of the Reform Act were framed not by Lord John Russell and the Whigs but by the Marquis of Blandford and a section of the disaffected Tory right. In 1829 and 1830 Blandford played his populist card and moved a number of bills. That of February 1830 proposed to abolish all rotten boroughs, transferring their seats to the counties and larger towns, a maximum parliamentary life of five years, payment for MPs, a householder franchise in the boroughs and an extension of the vote to copyholders in the counties. The Dissenting radical MP William Smith, responding in the Commons to Blandford's first initiative, gleefully asserted that Catholic emancipation 'appeared to have transformed a number of the highest Tories in the land to something very nearly resembling radical reformers' (7, p. 400).

Blandford's schemes had no chance of success. Whig reformers, though surprised by the speedy turn of events, would not be lured into supporting the Ultras. Many of them anyway considered that the extensions of the franchise proposed by

Blandford went much too far. His bill gained only 57 votes in the Commons; 160 voted against. Many Whigs prudently abstained. Russell, abandoning his commitment of four years earlier not to touch reform again, produced a much more modest proposal which was defeated by only 48 votes.

By early 1830, therefore, and by a series of events over which the Whigs had little or no influence, reform had returned to the political agenda. Many recent political historians argue that it had done so because the Tories splintered over religion. Many of the more Liberal Tories, originally associated with Canning, were now much closer to the Whigs than to Wellington, while on the right only recrimination and bile was to be encountered: little steady support could be expected from that quarter. Without some Whig support in February 1830 – provided in recognition of what was seen to be a principled stand over Catholic emancipation – Wellington's government would have failed to carry the king's speech at the beginning of the new parliamentary session. By July, the Ultra-Tory Duke of Newcastle confided in his diary that 'a weaker and more incapable ministry never sat in a Cabinet' (21, p. 255). The case for considering parliamentary reform the product of internecine Tory warfare at Westminster appears to be a strong one.

7

The crisis of 1830–2: a 'safe and practical' measure of reform?

The older case for considering parliamentary reform as the product of long-term radical dissatisfaction with the old political order is challenged by recent interpretations but not destroyed by them. The very different reform bills proposed by Blandford and Russell in 1829–30 were certainly not a response to extra-parliamentary pressure but such pressure was building up and would transform the situation over the next few months.

As ever, economic distress promoted political causes. The 1829 harvest failed, pushing up food prices. At the same time unemployment was on the increase in the cities. William Cobbett, the veteran reformer, who had defied anyone 'to agitate a fellow on a full stomach', saw that bellies were emptying. He returned to his pungent blend of journalistic rhetoric, reminding his readers, as he had told them in 1816, that the real cause of the people's distress was misgovernment. A landowners' parliament was wasting the nation's taxes on lavish expenditure, patronage and corruption.

The alliance between middle classes and working classes, essential for the success of any extra-parliamentary campaign, was much more extensively developed between 1829 and 1832 than ever before. In January 1830 the radical Birmingham banker, Thomas Attwood, formed a 'General Political Union between the Lower and the Middle classes of the people' in that city. Its purpose was to agitate for reform. During 1830, the

45

Birmingham example was followed in most other cities, despite the obvious economic differences which separated millowners and workforces in south Lancashire and the West Riding of Yorkshire. The precise objectives of many unions were deliberately fudged, since working-class leaders naturally favoured full male suffrage while their middle-class allies still distrusted democracy. But, for the moment, the fact of a workable alliance proved more important than the disagreements over strategy. In 1830 and 1831 the political unions were able to assemble a powerful engine of non-violent agitation: political rallies, demonstrations and a fusillade of reform petitions. As an anti-aristocratic movement especially strong in the unprecedentedly influential industrial areas of Britain, it dwarfed anything hitherto seen.

These developments were greeted with increasing nervousness at Westminster. Politicians had long recognized the growing importance of the middle classes. The working classes on their own, they judged, could still be defied, but in alliance with the middle classes they were unstoppable. Nervousness gave way to alarm in July 1830 when a rebellion in Paris overthrew the anti-reformist French king, Charles X, installed Louis Philippe and initiated a programme of reforms which briefly threatened to disturb the tranquillity of Europe. The July Revolution was an uneasy reminder of the events of 1789.

Before parliament had time to draw breath, agricultural labourers in Kent, weakened and demoralized by harvest failures and a shortage of jobs, had begun to burn hayricks in a series of outbreaks (the 'Swing Riots') which continued from August 1830 to December 1831. Some landowners feared that if agricultural workers, normally the most docile and least politically conscious of folk, were taking the law into their own hands then the entire fabric of society was at risk. The problem now was that, whereas in the 1790s and as late as 1819, MPs had rightly believed that law and order could be preserved by a series of repressive statutes and some well-publicized treason trials, evidence was now mounting that a similar remedy in 1830–1 might spark off a full-scale rebellion. MPs therefore began seriously to contemplate concessions. Was the granting of parliamentary reform the only way to avoid revolution? It cannot be denied that an increasing number of landowners and men of influence were fearful that political stability could not be maintained without what the Whigs began to call 'effective reform'. However important the problems of the Tory party at the time (see Chapter 6 above), extra-parliamentary agitation was concentrating more influential minds upon the necessity for reform by mid-1830 than ever before.

The death of George IV in June 1830 further weakened Wellington's position. The new king, William IV, had spent much of his life away from political affairs and came to kingship with few preconceptions. The diarist Greville famously, if exaggeratedly, described his prior existence as 'passed in obscurity and neglect. . . . Nobody ever invited him into their house, or thought it necessary to honour him with any mark of attention or respect' (37, p. 1). George would have found it very difficult to stomach a Whig ministry; when the time came William did not.

Nor did the general election which George's death required offer the Tories any comfort. It was not that the election destroyed Wellington's majority at a stroke – unreformed elections were not like that. Too few contests took place to make a total change in political complexion likely, and government influence in many Cornish boroughs and in Scotland remained strong. Yet, traditionally, general elections had strengthened the government's hand. The last important election, that of 1784, had given the new prime minister, Pitt, a parliamentary majority which he had previously lacked. Wellington looked similarly to the 1830 election to improve his position, but he was sorely disappointed. An attempt to unseat members of the Canning-Huskisson wing of the Tory party failed dismally. Party managers ruefully recognized that government patronage no longer carried its old weight. Notable government supporters, such as John Wilson Croker and Peel's brother Jonathan, were defeated. Where contests were held in the larger constituencies, those brave enough to declare themselves to be against reform were resoundingly beaten. Long-standing anti-reformers such as Thomas Gooch, a Suffolk MP since 1806, and E. P. Bastard, whose family had held one of the two Devon county seats without a break since 1784, were beaten. Most spectacularly, at the prompting of Edward Baines, editor of the *Leeds Mercury*, the radical lawyer Henry Brougham, took on and beat the Whig establishment in the county seat of Yorkshire. This was a real reversal of aristocratic fortunes. Yorkshire was a high electoral prize; for its large electorate to bestow victory on a man with no previous connections in the county spoke volumes about the extent of anti-aristocratic opinion in the country as a whole. Landowners needed no reminding that the political unions pitched their appeal at the productive elements in society, as against the idle and unproductive who inherited their wealth and lived off rent, the tribute of other men's labour. Victories such as Brougham's and the less publicized but in some ways even more startling, if temporary, defeat of the reformist aristocrat Lord John Russell at Bedford showed which way the wind was blowing. Russell's father bluntly blamed 'anti-aristocratical feelings' (24, p. 48).

The chief messages of the 1830 general election were that the old aristocratic system was unpopular as never before and that change was welcomed. Few candidates thought it wise to campaign actively for the old order. The reluctant conclusion that only reform could reduce hostility towards the aristocracy was increasingly widely shared. Lord Wharncliffe expressed his opinion to Wellington a little later: 'The demonstration in favour of Reform at the general election of 1830 satisfied me that the feeling upon it was not . . . temporary and likely to die away.' The election had three critical effects: it gravely weakened Wellington's government; it demonstrated the vote-winning possibilities of reform even among the restricted pre-1832 electorate; and it convinced remaining Whig doubters that support for reform was their best prospect of a return to power after a generation of opposition.

The election took place in July and August. Wellington's administration staggered on, demoralized and rudderless, until parliament reassembled in November. In the meantime popular agitation had increased in intensity. Southern and eastern hayricks continued to be burnt; radicals in the north and Midlands used the example of France to advance the cause of democracy; the situation was further complicated by industrial unrest among Lancashire cotton spinners and South Wales miners during October.

In November 1830 Wellington, taunted by Grey's homilies that concessions on reform were the only route to political salvation, made his famous, ill-fated response. The Lords were solemnly told that the prime minister

was fully convinced that the country possessed at the present

48

moment a legislature which answered all the good purposes of legislation, and this to a greater degree than any legislature ever had answered in any country whatever. He would go further and say that the legislature and the system of representation possessed the full and entire confidence of the country.

Wellington, having bent on Catholic emancipation to his great personal embarrassment, remained ramrod straight against political reform.

This spectacular piece of political misjudgement had precisely the opposite consequence of that intended. Wellington had hoped to stiffen the resolve of his supporters; instead he made them more fearful of the effects of continued resistance. Aberdeen briskly told Wellington when he sat down after making his speech: 'You have announced the fall of your government.' The prophecy was validated within a fortnight. The Huskissonite Tories finally made common cause with the Whigs and Wellington resigned after defeat on a finance measure. His ministers, in general, were glad to relinquish the burdens of office.

No alternative Tory administration was available to the king. So Earl Grey, who as Charles Grey had been ridiculed for pressing the reform issue in a hostile parliament in 1793, became prime minister 37 years later at the head of a Whig government finally convinced that parliamentary reform was no longer a divisive party issue. As we have seen (Chapter 6) Grey had not maintained an unswerving determination to champion parliamentary reform during the long intervening period but the reform which his government now sought to pilot through parliament bore striking resemblances to the proposals of the Friends of the People in the early 1790s (see pp. 24–5).

A ministerial committee under Lord Durham wrestled with the complexities of contending reform proposals during the winter of 1830–1. Lord John Russell, by now a veteran in such matters, was charged with the task of presenting a bill for which there was at last a prospect of success. Grey's aims underlay the specific proposals: the measure must be 'large enough to satisfy public opinion and to afford sure ground of resistance to further innovation'. No one should expect the Whigs to be democrats; they were aristocratic, and Grey's Cabinet of 1830 was one of the most blue-blooded in the nineteenth century. Grey realized, however, that mere tinkering with the existing system would not satisfy the much-heightened public expectation.

In January 1831 Durham's committee proposed to the Cabinet a scheme which was a curious mixture of the bold and the timid. Most surprisingly, it recommended a secret ballot, but proposed to reduce the effects of such audacity by establishing a standard qualification for a borough vote at the forbiddingly high level of property worth at least £20 a year. Such a provision would have reduced many existing electorates substantially; Bristol's, for example, would have been cut by about a half. More predictably, Durham proposed to disfranchise 61 boroughs entirely and to remove one of the two members from 47 more. Most of the seats would go to the counties and industrial towns, but the opportunity would be taken to reduce the size of the Commons from 658 members to 596.

These proposals were not submitted to public debate but were scrutinized in some detail within the Whig hierarchy. The ministry was by no means uniformly zealous in support of parliamentary reform. Melbourne, Lansdowne and Palmerston were all lukewarm at best. They urged greater caution and would have nothing to do with a secret ballot. However, Grey was able to use his authority to persuade them to substitute a £10 household franchise for the £20 one. Grey was convinced that public opinion would tolerate no higher threshold and it was a substantial hurdle. Nor was the proposal to compensate dispossessed borough owners for their loss considered tactful in a reforming adminstration. So, some hasty redrafting of the Durham committee recommendations was necessary before Russell could present the government's proposals to the Commons in March 1831. The proposals caused uproar in the House. MPs who had been in the House for any length of time had grown accustomed to Russell's measured proposals to disfranchise some rotten boroughs and transfer seats to the larger towns and the counties. In consequence they had discounted anything significantly more radical. Greville reported that the House found the Bill 'a sweeping measure indeed, much more so than anyone had imagined, because the Ministers had said it was one which would give *general* satisfaction, whereas this must dissatisfy all the moderate'. Outside parliament the general reaction was one of relief that a government had at last grasped the nettle. Attwood was confident that the proposals would not endanger his newly forged alliance between the middle and working classes. Many working-class leaders were temporarily dazzled by proposals for a uniform franchise. Henry Hetherington, editor of a new publication *Poor Man's Guardian*, whose central campaigning platform was universal manhood suffrage, was one of relatively few who saw the real implications of the £10 borough franchise. It would give the vote to small shopkeepers and tradesmen whilst withholding it from most working men. He was perceptive enough to appreciate that few sectors of society were more hostile to working-class political representation than the lower middle classes, on the well-established principle that those one rung further up any ladder are the most fearful of clamouring feet immediately below. Thus, while Bronterre O'Brien and John Doherty urged working people to support the bill as a necessary first instalment to the reform from which they would directly benefit, Hetherington counselled opposition on the grounds that it would be used not to foster but to block more radical change later.

The parliamentary debates produced some closely argued contributions on both sides. It is interesting to notice, however, that within parliament the pro-reformers tended to take a more pragmatic stance while the anti-reformers invoked principle and ancient precedent. It was common ground on both sides that democracy was to be avoided at all costs. Russell spoke for most MPs when he argued in a speech made in the Commons a few months before the Whigs came into office: 'Universal suffrage and vote by ballot are measures that, in my opinion, are incompatible with the Constitution of this country.' He looked rather to what he called 'safe and practical reform'. The Whigs, therefore, looked to produce a reform which would strengthen the existing social and political order whereas Tory opponents believed that any change would weaken that order. The debate within parliament was, in truth, more about means than ends.

T. B. Macaulay from the Whig side argued the necessity to attach the middle classes firmly to the existing constitution by including them in it:

We say, and we say justly, that it is not by mere numbers, but by property and intelligence that the nation ought to be governed. Yet, saying this, we exclude from all share in the government vast masses of property and intelligence – vast numbers of those who are most interested in preserving tranquillity, and who know best how to preserve it.

The Tory writer John Wilson Croker pointed out that proposals which he believed would subvert the constitution also contained contradictions and anomalies which would invalidate it even on its own terms. Sir Robert Inglis, MP for Oxford University, concentrated on the dangers of novelty and on the tried and tested virtues of the existing system: 'the charge I bring against [the Bill is of its] being a rash and untried theory, of being a vain and unsubstantial speculation, of being founded upon no precedent which ever existed in this country'. The House of Commons, he asserted, had always been able to adapt to change; thus it 'is now, [as] it has been for a long succession years: it is the most complete representation of the interests of the people, which was ever assembled in any age or country'.

Sir Robert Peel probably knew that some measure of parliamentary reform was inevitable. However, he could not afford to support even this modest measure since it would involve flouting Ultra opinion on reform in 1831 or 1832 as well as on religion in 1829 (see above, pp. 42–3). His future, he calculated, lay in maintaining an anti-reform stance. Thus he was to be found echoing Pitt in 1793: 'Let us never be tempted to resign the well tempered freedom which we enjoy, in the ridiculous pursuit of the wild liberty which France has established . . . liberty which has neither justice nor wisdom for its companions.'

Grey was dismayed by the tenacity of his opponents. His bill passed its second reading stage by a single vote (302 to 301) on 22 March in the biggest parliamentary division ever recorded. Such a narrow victory, far less than had been predicted, was quite insufficient to guard against damaging amendments as the bill trundled through discussion in committee. In a wider context, however, Grey could draw comfort from the composition of his victory. County members voted for the reform by a majority of two to one; borough members whose seats would remain after 1832 voted for it in almost an equal proportion; the Irish supported it by about three to two proportionally. An appeal to the electorate would stand an excellent chance of strengthening his hand.

So, when the first adverse amendment was carried in committee, Grey persuaded a most reluctant William IV to break with convention and dissolve parliament after less than a year. The elections of April/May 1831 were a huge triumph for the reformers. They won almost all the 'open' boroughs. Only 6 of the 34 county MPs who had voted against reform either on second reading or in the critical amendment got back to parliament. Grey had a majority in excess of 130 seats in the Commons after an election which became virtually a plebiscite on reform.

But the Commons was not synonymous with parliament. In the House of Lords an intractable anti-reform majority remained, unelected and apparently immovable. It is an interesting commentary on radical reformers that they paid little attention to the House of Lords, believing with Paine that the Lords would wither away once reform of the lower house was accomplished. The events of the next few months showed what an obstacle the Lords could be. If reform were to be carried 'by due process of law', then that process necessitated majorities in both houses of parliament. The Lords could exercise an absolute veto on even the largest Commons majority.

A large Commons majority was not long in coming. In July 1831 a second Reform Bill, very similar to the first, passed through the Commons with a majority of almost 140. The committee stage involved some intricate horse trading in which some boroughs were given reprieves and other new towns enfranchised. The only important change was that introduced by Lord Chandos, who carried an amendment to enfranchise county tenants renting property worth at least £50 a year. The change could be justified on grounds of providing an extension of county voters parallel with that provided for the boroughs but, as we shall see (pp. 61–2), it had important political implications.

The bill arrived in the Lords on 22 September 1831. In the early hours of 8 October, after a fiery debate, they threw it out by a majority of 41. Later that same day, riots broke out in Derby and Nottingham and during the rest of the month extensive rioting was experienced both in large towns, most notably Bristol, and in small ones like the west of England woollen towns, Blandford and Tiverton. In towns which did not riot, new political unions were formed or existing ones strengthened; mass meetings and processions were held; vitriolic anti-aristocratic resolutions were passed by acclamation. Hostility was directed also against the hierarchy of the Church of England since of 26 bishops who sat in the Lords, 21 had voted with the majority. Had they voted otherwise, a reform act would have been passed in 1831.

Britain has never in modern times been closer to revolution than in the autumn of 1831. Princess Lieven, the wife of the Russian ambassador and an astute observer of the British political scene, had written to her brother a year earlier on the fall of Wellington: 'We too, in England, are just on the brink of a revolution' (37, p. 29). The assessment then was certainly overdramatic, but by October 1831 many more were prepared to believe it. Cabinet members seriously doubted whether the archaic system of national defence could withstand the strains now put upon it. With the partial exception of London, after Peel's experiment in 1829, no police force yet existed. The army was neither large enough nor trained enough to cope with widespread rioting. At his country seat, Drayton Manor, Peel laid in quantities of arms to withstand a possible siege by Staffordshire rioters. Possibly, only the government's professed determination to continue with reform prevented a grand explosion.

The riots, in addition to thoroughly alarming the authorities, did emphasize one standing weakness of the extra-parliamentary reformers, namely that the middle classes did not riot in October 1831. Indeed, many small shopkeepers feared for their own property and, at least temporarily, placed a higher priority on law and order than they did on reform. The latent hostility between middle classes and working classes surfaced. Thomas Attwood, seeing the danger, helped to keep the reform forces more or less together with an ambiguous call to the middle classes to arm themselves. While Grey and the Whigs could take this as further evidence of the pro-reform determination of the middle classes, many small tradesmen were only too happy to obey Attwood's call – but to defend themselves against 'the rabble'.

The Whigs meanwhile sought ways of overthrowing the anti-reform majority in the Lords. When Russell presented the third reform bill to the Commons in December, substantial changes had been made to the list of boroughs scheduled to lose one of their two members. These were reduced in number from 41 to 30 and ten proposed new boroughs were now given not one member, but two. The Commons majority, unimportantly, moved up to 162. The battle was to take place in the Lords. Many ministers, led by Durham, were convinced that the constitutional *impasse* could be resolved only by the creation of sufficient new peers known to favour reform to outvote the anti-reformers. But William IV, who regarded such a manoeuvre as both a constitutional and a social outrage, would have to be coerced. Grey counselled caution, urging that the mere threat to dilute blue blood to a turquoise rinse would be enough. For the moment, ministers left matters as they were, and were rewarded in April 1832 with a Lords majority of nine in favour of the new bill. Further consultations with opposition leaders followed in the hope of avoiding defeats in committee. Grey was even prepared to reprieve more boroughs and restrict the number of new industrial seats, but to no avail. A wrecking amendment was carried in the first week of May. Grey rushed to the king to demand fifty new peers immediately. The king refused to be hurried: Grey tendered his resignation.

So began the crisis known as the 'Days of May'. William IV asked Wellington to investigate the possibility of forming a ministry which would promote a more modest Reform Bill. Wellington, as opposed to reform as ever, but finally appreciating that in some form it must come, agreed to try. Predominantly Tory peers might be persuaded to pass a Tory reform measure when they had been reluctant to pass a Whig one.

Extra-parliamentary hostility, which had provoked the Reform Crisis, now had a further say in determining its outcome. Thomas Attwood and Francis Place, 'the radical tailor of Charing Cross' who had enjoyed a long career of reforming political manipulation beginning with the London Corresponding Society in the 1790s, organized yet more demonstrations, now of hostility to Wellington. Westminster was flooded with anti-Tory petitions. Forms of middle-class coercion were canvassed. Property owners should withhold taxes. More subtly, Place suggested that investors should all withdraw their assets from the banks at once, precipitating a financial on top of a political crisis: 'To stop the Duke', ran the slogan, 'go for Gold.' *The Times* reported on 15 and 16 May that the message was having some effect:

The counter in the Cashier's office, at which sovereigns are obtained, was beset during the whole day with applicants, chiefly in sums varying from £20 to £100, besides which large amounts have been drawn out by the private bankers . . . in anticipation of a general demand for gold under the present excitement which prevails (37, p. 125).

Loose talk of armed resistance was bandied about, though the nation as a whole was less frenzied than it had been in October 1831 and Wellington's ability to form a government had yet to be tested.

In the event, he failed. This was largely because Peel, much the most substantial Tory figure in the Commons and more from reasons of political calculation than principle, refused to be a member of any government committed to bringing in reform. He believed that he could not again cross the Ultras on a major measure so soon after his 'betrayal' over Catholic emancipation. He nurtured growing hopes of leading his party and aspirant leaders are usually accommodating to those they disagree with but whose support they need. Once Peel had refused to serve, Wellington informed the king that he was unable to form a government. Four tortured days later, William swallowed his pride and asked Grey, whose tendered resignation he had not formally accepted, to take again the reins of government with the critical promise that he would, when necessary, create sufficient peers to bludgeon the Lords into submission.

The need for extra peers never came. Parliamentary opposition collapsed once Wellington confessed defeat. Most of the peers who had frustrated Grey in May absented themselves from the upper house when, on 4 June, the third reading of the third Reform Bill was passed by 106 votes to 22. Popular agitation was quietened. Perhaps fortunately for them, Place and Attwood had no need to make good their threats of civil disruption. We can never know what would have happened if the Lords had called the radicals' bluff and kept to their anti-reforming principles. Nothing is more certain, however, than that reform was peacefully enacted in June 1832 not because noble lords were persuaded by the merits of the case, but because they feared the consequences of continued resistance.

8

How much was changed by the Reform Act of 1832, and in whose interest?

In this chapter, frequent reference is made to the specific changes brought about by the Reform Act. These are itemized in the Appendices, which should be consulted alongside the text.

Evaluating the importance of the first Reform Act has been hampered by two opposing over-simplifications. Historians writing in the early twentieth century took the importance of the Reform Act for granted. As the leading student of the topic at that time put it, the Act saw the 'feet of the nation being placed in the direction of democracy' (3). It enfranchised the majority of the middle classes and, despite the best intentions of the Whigs, it opened the door for further, and more dramatic, changes. The over-simplification of this view is that the Act was responsible for making the middle classes the rulers of Britain. In 1832, they entered the political kingdom, in appropriate recognition of their industrial and commercial might. In fact, the middle classes were no more the rulers of Britain in, say, 1860 than they had been in 1830. Palmerston's and even Gladstone's Cabinets in the second half of the nineteenth century were just as aristocratic as was Grey's in 1830 and the prime minister at the turn of the twentieth century was the Earl of Salisbury, head of one of the country's most senior aristocratic families. The reasons for relatively limited middle-class influence at Westminster are examined later in this chapter.

Recognition that the 1832 Reform Act made no dramatic

changes to the personnel of government has led to an equally misleading myth at the other extreme. Over-stressing themes of continuity before and after 1832 can lead to the conclusion that the Act was a measure of little significance, its importance grossly exaggerated by contemporaries both within parliament and in the nation at large. It is, of course, perfectly true, as Professor Hanham says (29) that the Act 'was in no sense a revolutionary measure'. It was not intended to be. Henry Hetherington, editor of *Poor Man's Guardian*, published an article on the real significance of the Act in October 1832. It summed up what he believed ought to be working-class frustration at a measure which aimed to shore up the old system largely by excluding working people:

> with a little instinctive sense of self-preservation, have the Whigs manufactured a 'great measure'. They know that the old system could not last and desiring to establish another as like it as possible, and also to keep their places, they framed a Bill, in the hope of drawing to the feudal aristocracy and yeomanry of the counties a large reinforcement of the middle class. The Bill was, in effect, an invitation to the shopocrats of the enfranchised towns to join the Whigocrats of the country, and make common cause with them in keeping down the people, and thereby quell the rising spirit of democracy in England.

It should not be argued, however, that a Bill which detached the middle classes from their working-class allies had all the conservative consequences which its framers hoped for. As was argued in Chapter 1, the Reform Act must be studied in its broader context. It set in motion far more than the Whigs anticipated. Its true significance can be appreciated only by studying longer-term, as well as immediate, consequences.

The precise terms of the Act, particularly the list of boroughs disfranchised and replaced, were the result of compromises made at the height of the crisis of 1831–2. The general strategy of reform, however, was clear enough and the 1832 Act did not betray it. Grey told the Lords in 1831 that 'The principle of my reform is, to prevent the necessity for revolution . . . there is no one more dedicated against annual parliaments, universal suffrage, and the ballot, than I am.' This was no window dressing by a politician anxious to extract votes from a hostile audience.

Grey believed in 1831, as in 1793, that moderate reform was the only secure route to political stability. He would not abandon the principle of aristocratic government; rather the Whigs would strengthen it by attaching to the existing constitution the new forms of propertied interest. What Grey and the Whigs wished to preserve above all things was the continuance of government by men of property. Absolutely no contradiction existed between the preservation of property rights and a considerable extension of the franchise.

The Whigs aimed to frustrate democracy by increasing the franchise. The paradox in this is only superficial. Many of those enfranchised for the first time in 1832 were small property owners. Appendix 2 indicates how significant the increase in the number of voters was. The electorate increased from about one in eight adult males to just short of one in five. In Scotland (Appendix 1b) the prospect of genuine tests of propertied opinion appeared for the first time in 1832, even though only one man in eight there had the vote. Ireland, of course, had a more restricted county electorate (Appendix 1c) since it was deemed unwise to enfranchise large numbers of Catholic peasants. Only 5 per cent of Irishmen were entitled to vote after 1832.

It is frequently forgotten that the electorate continued to increase *between* the first and second Reform Acts. Increased prosperity, the effects of gentle inflation and efficient electoral registration combined to raise the electorate in England and Wales from about 650,000 in 1833 to just over a million in 1866 (Appendix 2). This more than offset the reductions caused by the deaths of poorer men who had been entitled to vote before 1832 and thus retained that right during their lifetimes. Overall, the consequence of change between the Reform Acts was slightly to increase the proportion of men entitled to vote, from about 18 per cent to about 20 per cent (Appendix 2).

There is little doubt that the Whigs acted as they did for two main reasons. First, leading figures like Grey retained some kind of pride in the feeling that they were the party of change and, within limits, of trust in the people. Second, and more importantly, they were persuaded of the need to make concessions to counter growing frustration with the existing system (see Chapters 6 and 7). Only two significant attempts have been made to deny that the Whigs' prime motive was concessionary. Karl

Marx in the middle of the nineteenth century argued that the Whigs had calculated finely that the changes would increase their own electoral influence at the expense of the Tories'. Thus, the Whigs' main motivation was party advantage. Marx was wrong: some Whigs saw much more acutely than Marx that the main electoral beneficiaries within a few years were likely to be the Tories. As in so much else, both Marx's analysis – though original – and his predictions proved faulty.

In the mid-1970s, Professor D. C. Moore, in an over-long and turgid book entitled *The Politics of Deference*, argued that MPs used the opportunities created by the political crises of 1830–2 not so much to make concessions to extra-parliamentary pressure but to cure a damaging imbalance in the existing constitution. According to Moore, the real intention of 1832 was not to increase the franchise but to redraw constituency boundaries. Most electors, he argued, voted the way their betters wanted and advised. This being so, it would be valuable to ensure that these 'betters' represented clearly defined separate, rather than mixed, interests. Those urban interests and values which had been dangerously seeping into many county seats (see Chapter 2), could now be confined to their proper, and appropriately limited, sphere. The landed interest would thus exercise unchallenged sway in an expanded rural electorate.

The idea of an electoral *cordon sanitaire* around, say, Bradford or Birmingham is an intriguing one and doubtless of some attraction to those of more refined aesthetic sensibility. Unfortunately, as a prime objective for passing a Reform Act Moore's argument fails the crucial test of evidence. As with so many plausible sociological theories, how things *might* ideally operate takes precedence over how they actually *do*. Professor Moore's views have found almost no support among historians and it seems safe to consign his 'cure' thesis to the capacious compartment of failed theories. Parliament passed the 1832 Reform Act because it feared the consequences of not doing so. Althorp spoke for most Whigs in November 1831 in the wake of the Lords' rejection of the bill. It must be re-presented, he told Lord Stanley, and the government's task was clear: 'the bill at last must be carried by force or fear, not from conviction or affection' (**24**, p. 63). He was referring, of course, to reactions in the Lords not in the country as a whole.

The purpose of a uniform £10 borough qualification (Appendix 1) was twofold. It kept out non-property owners, who were deemed unworthy to be trusted with the vote, and it made a move to replace the chaos of borough franchises which had been so evident before 1832. The precise effects of the change differed markedly across the country since rental values varied. In London, where they were high, many skilled workers with permanent residences qualified; in Cornwall and parts of Wales, where they were very low, even some shopkeepers were kept off the voting roll. In the Midland and northern towns, on whose representation so much discussion had centred, the qualification was intentionally stiff. In Leeds, for example, a city of some 125,000 people in 1831 a high proportion of whom were industrial workers, only 5,000 people were entitled to vote in 1832. Birmingham had approximately 7,000 houses worth £10 a year in a total population of 144,000 and Manchester about 13,000 in a population of 182,000. In some constituencies, such as Preston, Coventry and Westminster where the pre-1832 franchise had been wide and many artisans and craftsmen had been able to vote (Chapter 2), numbers actually declined as old voters died. In Lancaster, about 2,500 people voted in the election of 1831. By 1851, the number was reduced (mostly by death) to 1,400. Not only larger boroughs were affected. No doubt in part due to family pressure, the Peel family borough of Tamworth survived the axe in 1832, when it had 528 electors. By 1852, this number had shrunk to 307.

In the counties, much controversy attended the passage of the Chandos amendment which enfranchised tenants. The amendment increased the county electorate by about 30 per cent more than the Whigs intended and it was contentious because it was feared that a move, superficially in the direction of greater representation, would actually increase the influence of the aristocracy. Since 1832 brought no secret ballot (Appendix 4), it was feared that landlords would tell tenants whom to vote for, on pain of eviction when their leases expired. The possibilities of influence undoubtedly existed. Landlords could also increase forty-shilling freeholds to enable more people to vote on their behalf. But such methods proved only minor factors in the continued influence of landowners over the political system. Landowners and their agents were men of business and agriculture had become a highly profit-conscious enterprise. Proprietors would lose more than they would gain by evicting politically hostile tenants for the sake of a few extra votes if those tenants were good farmers. It was true, however, that most of these new county voters were of the same political persuasion as their landlords. After 1832, farmers were overwhelmingly Tory. The Tory revival of the 1830s and early 1840s was based, not so much on Peel's alleged 'modernization' of his party, but upon the Tory loyalism of the tenantry. In Peel's famous general election victory of 1841, the Tories actually lost ground in the largest boroughs but they won the 159 English and Welsh county seats in the proportion 137 to 22.

The registration of voters (Appendix 1) had extremely important political consequences. After 1832, it was not enough for a potential elector to satisfy the property qualification; he must get himself onto the electoral register. The number of houses rated at £10 or more is not always a reliable guide to the number of electors since, in the nineteenth century as in the twentieth, by no means all potential voters expressed enthusiasm for the political process. The emergence of the local party agent was the natural consequence. Good agents proved themselves worth their weight in gold. They tramped the streets ascertaining where support lay among prospective voters and then guided those voters through the sometimes complex registration process in the Revising Barrister's Court.

Obviously, it was to a party's advantage to get as many of its own supporters on to the register as possible and, by arguing cases in the Revising Courts, to deny as many opponents as could be managed. In the early years after 1832 it was the Tory party which the better manipulated what Peel rightly called 'a perfectly new element of political power'. Professional agents were appointed in most of the large towns and became the vanguard of modern party-political organization. The Tories won a famous election victory in 1841 and, though many textbooks have concentrated on Whig shortcomings in office, at least as much attention should be paid to the efficiency of Tory party organization in the boroughs. When both parties were well organized in the 1860s, the new registration system permitted a realistic assessment to be made of the numbers entitled to vote. In the 1830s and 1840s the composition of a borough list often tells more about the strength of the respective party organizations. Since many dead men 'voted' in the early years while others were prevented from doing so by various subterfuges at which agents rapidly became adept, it might be said that the Reform Act actually added new potential for manipulation.

The old means of corruption were not eliminated in 1832. Bribing and treating of voters continued. A committee under the Marquis of Hartington reported in 1870 (after the passage of the second Reform Act) that 'a considerable class of voters will not vote unless they are paid'. Lancaster, St Albans and Totnes all had reputations for notorious corruption. Rioting and revelling at election times were not unknown in Victorian England. Indeed, since more contests took place after 1832 opportunities for corruption may even have increased. Between 1784 and 1831 roughly 30 per cent of seats were actually contested; in the elections between the first and second Reform Acts, 52.5 per cent of seats went to the polls.

The lack of legislation to eliminate electoral 'influence' after 1832 (Appendix 4) is quite deliberate. Any move towards 'fairer' elections or equal electoral districts could be interpreted as a dangerous compromise with the principles of democracy. In preparing the list of enfranchised and disfranchised boroughs, Russell was careful to inform the Commons in 1831, the government

> had never put the measure of Reform on a footing of such perfect symmetry and regularity as to reduce the Representation of the country to exact proportions . . . anomalies they found, and anomalies, though not such glaring ones as now existed, they meant to leave.

So boroughs like Thetford, Reigate, Westbury and Calne survived in 1832 although none had more than 200 voters. Croydon, Doncaster and Loughborough had populations in excess of 10,000 in 1831, but were not dignified with a parliamentary seat. County representation in England was increased by 59 seats, but the counties were still numerically under-represented with 57 per cent of the electorate, and only 32 per cent of the seats.

'Managed' or 'pocket' boroughs also survived, though in reduced numbers. Professor Gash estimates that between 60 and 70 MPs continued to fill parliamentary seats because of patronage (23). Pocket boroughs did have some intrinsic merit. They did allow able, but inevitably well-connected, men to enter parliament very young and thus to build long careers in the service of the nation: the parliaments elected after 1832 still had a large proportion of men in their twenties. No less than 36 per cent of members of the Commons of 1841–7 had been first elected before they reached their thirtieth birthdays. One of these was William Ewart Gladstone, who came from a very prosperous commercial family in Liverpool: he had been recommended to the Duke of Newcastle as a likely young man and firm in the Tory interest. The Duke presented him to the borough of Newark in Nottinghamshire whose electors duly returned him to the first reformed parliament in December 1832; Gladstone was just short of 23 years old. Gladstone's immensely long parliamentary career, most of it subsequently in the Liberal party, began in the new House in exactly the same way as had those of Pitt the Younger and Charles James Fox in the old: selected for a pocket borough almost as soon as he came of age. It is not so surprising that Gladstone, as late as 1859 and with his anti-reform period some years behind him, should still be found defending pocket boroughs. He favoured the creation of a wider electorate but he argued that a new reform bill could accommodate a few 'managed' seats. 'You cannot expect of large and populous constituencies that they return boys to Parliament; and yet, if you want a succession of men trained to take part in the government, you must have a great proportion of them returned to the House while they are boys.'

Continuity after 1832 went much further than the survival of a reduced number of managed boroughs. Effectively, the same people ruled Britain. Of those elected in December 1832, between 70 and 80 per cent represented the landed interest; the largest specific category was that comprising the sons of the peerage. Not more than 100 members were bankers, merchants or manufacturers. Many pre-1832 parliaments had returned similar numbers of the professional and industrial middle classes. Althorp's prediction in December 1831 that MPs 'would continue to be selected from the same classes as at present' proved accurate enough. Though the middle classes had the vote, they did not return a significantly larger number of middle-class MPs. A slow change set in from the 1840s but at least until the 1870s parliament remained in overall aristocratic control. Neither were radical MPs more numerous. Only 46 MPs could be persuaded by Attwood in July 1839 to vote even for consideration of the Chartist petition for universal manhood suffrage and five other democratic demands. Democracy continued to be a dirty word in the reformed Commons.

Why were the rising middle classes so poorly represented? The reasons are partly practical and partly psychological. Many businessmen were intensely interested in politics, but they found local questions far more rewarding. Between the 1830s and the 1860s much more attention was given in places like Leeds and Birmingham to issues such as local public health, education and civic amenities than to national politics. Local elections were contested with an intensity which late twentieth-century voters, generally too bored with them to vote at all, would find astounding. The Victorian city, however, symbolized modern civilization and its governance was a matter of first importance. Civic pride motivated men for whom parliament was remote not only geographically, but also to their immediate concerns. It should not be forgotten that mid-nineteenth-century governments exercised far less influence over local affairs than do the governments of today. For this reason, the Municipal Corporations Act (1835) deserves much more prominence than it normally receives in textbooks. This Act hastened the disappearance of large numbers of small, unrepresentative local vestries and their replacement by elected local councils. At these elections, rather than at those for Westminster, the middle classes fought among themselves as Whig-Liberals or as Conservatives. In doing so they greatly extended the power and influence of the industrial, commercial and professional interests. The reforms of the 1830s therefore, *did* increase the power of the middle classes, but not by the means usually identified.

Local communities retained much autonomy, but the government of an increasingly complex industrial society still required more parliamentary time than hitherto. Parliamentary sessions lengthened and, for the first time, MPs could choose to interpret their jobs as full-time ones. Since parliamentary duties remained unpaid (Appendix 4) only MPs of private means, or able to make money in London at times convenient for parliamentary sittings, such as lawyers and bankers, could afford the financial sacrifice required. Most men of private means had inherited wealth and most inherited wealth was landed in origin. A cotton manufacturer, unless his business was well established or his faith in his business partners total, needed to be near his mills. The landowner, and still more his sons, could leave day-to-day administration in the hands of agents. It is not surprising that parliament was still dominated by gentlemen of leisure.

The psychological reasons for the continuing landed dominance of parliament may be the most important of all. There is
little evidence to suggest that the middle classes were avid to
grasp political power. They demanded representation, taking
the view that the vote was more valuable as a privilege to be
won than as a 'right of man' to be demanded. Fundamentally,
most were as conservative as their social superiors. As Michael
Brock puts it, 'most of the new voters wanted not to challenge
the aristocracy, but to win recognition from it: once they had
their rightful position they did not favour further adventures'
(2, p. 319). It is one of the less endearing foibles of human
nature that most people can find reasons to attack clubs of
which they are not members. Once admitted to any privileged
circle, they can find good cause for defending the very institutions they once derided. As Grey had calculated, the middle
classes soon proved themselves a reassuringly conservative
force. Some of the most devastating attacks on the Chartist
democrats of the 1830s and 1840s came from those small
shopkeepers and tradesmen who ten years earlier had made
common cause with working men to alarm the establishment
into political reform.

The doom-laden prophecies of the Tory opponents of reform,
therefore, proved ludicrously wide of the mark. One of the most
prominent of them, the writer, MP and diarist John Wilson
Croker, had said that 'The reform Bill is a stepping stone in
England to a republic. The Bill once passed, goodnight to the
Monarchy, and the Lords and the Church.' Yet we still wait,
with no obvious signs of impatience, to bid adieu to any of
them. Wellington expected that 'we shall be destroyed one after
the other . . . by due course of law'. The old soldier lived for
twenty years after the passage of the Reform Act, most of them
spent still at the centre of politics. Had he been much given
to either reflection or introspection he would have recognized
the folly of this utterance long before his death.

What Grey and his colleagues had done was to forge the most
durable of political alliances, that between land and industry; it
would stand fast for many years against the assaults of the
democrats. It is no wonder that working-class leaders spoke so
bitterly about their old allies, the middle classes, after 1832. The
rights of property had been given a new lease of life, largely

under existing management. Britain, alone of the advanced nations of Western Europe, avoided political revolution in the 1830s and 1840s. European revolutions depended to a significant extent upon middle-class leadership. The middle classes in Britain had been hitched to the waggon of established authority. In the short term, the Reform Act strengthened the status quo.

But in the longer term, of course, the Reform Act opened the door to more dramatic changes, as Peel had feared it would. The 1832 Act could not be, as Lord John Russell had presented it, 'the final solution of a great constitutional question'. By 1848, Russell himself was convinced that a new dose of reform was necessary. Within thirty years, politicians recognized that they would have to trust working men with the vote. By the end of the century, it would not be a misnomer to talk of a middle-class dominated parliament. Soon enough, the aristocracy would have to share an influence which they had been used to exercising alone. But it would be a sharing of powers, however unequally and uneasily, not the crude supersession of one ruling class by another. This is the true measure of the 1832 Reform Act. For all its imperfections, it set a modern industrial state firmly on the path to gradual, non-violent change. That is why it deserves to be remembered as the pre-eminent piece of legislation in nineteenth-century Britain.

Appendix 1a
The 1832 Reform Act
(England and Wales)

Qualifications for the vote

IN COUNTY SEATS

  i Adult males owning freehold property worth at least 40 shillings (£2) per annum.

 ii Adult males in possession of a copyhold worth at least £10 per annum.

iii Adult males leasing or renting land worth at least £50 per annum. (This provision resulted from the 'Chandos Amendment'.)

IN BOROUGH SEATS

 i Adult males owning or occupying property worth at least £10 per annum provided:

   a that they had been in possession of the property for at least one year and had paid all taxes charged on that property;

   b that they had not been in receipt of parish poor relief during the previous year.

ii Voters who did not qualify under i but who had exercised a vote in a borough before 1832 retained the right to vote in that borough (unless, of course, the borough had disappeared under the Act) during their lifetimes, provided that they lived in, or within seven miles of, the borough where they would vote. This right to vote could not be passed on to heirs or successors.

Changes in the distribution of seats

IN ENGLAND

i 56 borough constituencies (cited as Schedule A boroughs in the Act) lost their representation entirely.
ii 30 boroughs (Schedule B) lost one of their two members.
iii 22 new parliamentary boroughs (Schedule C) created with two members.
iv 19 new parliamentary boroughs (Schedule D) created with one member.
v County representation increased. One county to have six members; 26 to have four members; 7 counties to have three members; 6 counties to retain two members; Isle of Wight to become a separate, single-member constituency.

IN WALES

i In the boroughs the old system of grouping boroughs retained but two new single-member boroughs created.
ii In the counties, three counties now returned two members; 9 counties continued to return one member each.

NB Specific changes itemized in Appendix 2.

Registration

A register of electors to be compiled in each constituency.

Appendix 1b
The 1832 Reform Act (Scotland)

Main qualifications for the franchise

COUNTIES

i All owners of property with a yearly value of at least £10.
ii Leaseholders to the value of £10 if on a lease for life or for not less than 57 years; leaseholders to the value of £50 on a lease for not less than 19 years.
iii Tenants of property worth £50.
iv Existing voters, not otherwise qualified, retained the right to vote during their lifetimes.

BURGHS

i All occupiers of property worth at least £10 per annum (same qualification as for England with same caveats on taxes and non-receipt of parochial relief).
ii The old system, whereby town councils elected a delegate who had one vote in election, abolished.

Changes in distribution of seats

COUNTIES

i 30 seats, as before. 27 countries to return one member each. Elgin & Nairn, Ross & Cromarty, Clackmannan and Kinross joined, each group electing one member.

BURGHS

i Representation increased from 15 to 23.
ii Edinburgh and Glasgow to return two members each; Aberdeen, Dundee, Greenock, Paisley and Perth to return one member each.
iii Remaining 14 seats to come from the system, retained from the old practice, of grouping individual burghs into districts, each of 14 districts to return one member.

Appendix 1c
The 1832 Reform Act (Ireland)

Main qualifications for the franchise

COUNTIES

i All owners of property with a yearly value of at least £10 (NB this was the same provision as had applied since Catholic emancipation in 1829).

ii Leaseholders to the value of £10 with leases of at least 20 years.

BOROUGHS

i All occupiers of property worth at least £10 per annum (as in England).

ii Some cities were legally considered as 'counties of cities'. Here the right to vote was extended to £10 freeholders and leaseholders.

iii Those entitled to vote before 1832 and not otherwise qualified retained the vote during their lifetime.

Distribution of seats

COUNTIES

Each of the 32 counties returned two members, as before.

i To the original 35 borough seats were added one extra member each for Belfast, Galway, Limerick and Waterford.

ii A second seat was given to the University of Dublin with a franchise extending to all holders of MA and higher degrees.

Appendix 2
Growth of the electorate in England and Wales, 1831–3 and 1833–66

	1831	1833	% Increase 1831–3	1866	% Increase 1833–66
Counties	239,000	370,379	55	543,633	47
Boroughs	200,000	282,398	41	514,026	82
Combined	439,000	652,777	49	1,056,659	62

The 1831 figures are estimates, based on the research of Frank O'Gorman. More detailed information about the pre-reform electorate will be found in his *Voters, Patrons and Parties: The Unreformed Electoral System of Hanoverian England, 1734–1832*. Earlier estimates, which put the pre-1832 electorate at 366,000, were based on those who actually voted in the elections, rather than on those entitled to vote. Thus, the 1832 Reform Act probably increased the electorate by less than 50 per cent rather than by almost 80 per cent as is generally held.

Estimated proportion of adult males entitled to vote in England and Wales

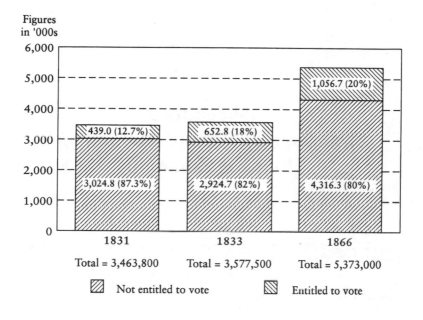

Figures in '000s

6,000

5,000 — — — — — — — — — — — — — — — —

1,056.7 (20%)

4,000 — — — — — — — — — — — — — — — —

439.0 (12.7%)   652.8 (18%)

3,000 — — — — — — — — — — — — — — — —

2,000 — — — — — — — — — — — — — — — —

3,024.8 (87.3%)   2,924.7 (82%)   4,316.3 (80%)

1,000 — — — — — — — — — — — — — — — —

0

1831   1833   1866

Total = 3,463,800   Total = 3,577,500   Total = 5,373,000

▨ Not entitled to vote   ▨ Entitled to vote

Appendix 3
The changed composition of the House of Commons

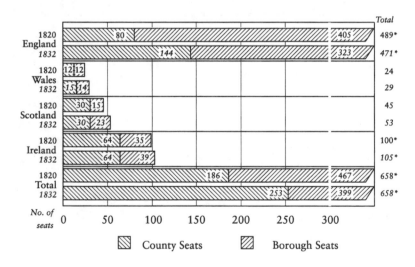

* Figure inclusive of University seats (4 for England pre- and post-1832; 1 for Ireland before 1832 and 2 after 1832)

1820 was chosen as an arbitrary, if convenient, pre-reform date since the 'rotten' Cornish borough of Grampound was disfranchised in 1826 and its two seats were transferred to Yorkshire, giving much the largest county in England four seats instead of the normal two.

Direct Scottish representation at Westminster dated from the Act of Union in 1707 and the 100 Irish members arrived in 1801 after the passing of the Anglo-Irish Act of Union the previous year.

Appendix 4
Major radical items
not conceded in 1832

  i No manhood suffrage. Universal male suffrage not achieved until 1918.
 ii No annually elected parliaments. Length of parliament remained a maximum of seven years until 1911, when this was reduced to five years.
iii A property qualification for MPs remained. The possession of property to the value of at least £300 a year was a minimum qualification until 1858.
 iv No payment of salaries to MPs. MPs remained unpaid until 1911.
  v No secret ballot. Voting remained public until 1872.

Select bibliography

The literature on parliamentary reform is vast. In what follows, I have tried to identify only those texts which are most important, and most accessible, for both teachers and students.

1 J. Cannon, *Parliamentary Reform, 1640–1832* (2nd edn, Cambridge, 1980)
2 M. Brock, *The Great Reform Act* (London, 1973)

These are now the standard works. However, for many purposes – not least a valuable and well-written narrative – the following work remains worth consulting:

3 J. R. M. Butler, *The Passing of the Great Reform Bill* (New York, 1914)

A lot of research has been done on the eighteenth-century electorate. It requires us to reconsider many of the generalizations about 'corruption' and lack of popular involvement in the political system:

4 F. O'Gorman, *Voters, Patrons and Parties: The Unreformed Electoral System of Hanoverian England, 1734–1832* (Oxford, 1989) – also contains an excellent bibliography of books and articles
5 F. O'Gorman, 'The unreformed electorate of Hanoverian England: The mid-18th century to 1832', *Social History*, Vol. 11 (1986), pp. 33–52
6 J. A. Phillips, *Electoral Behavior in Unreformed England* (Princeton, New Jersey, 1982)

The bold, Tory revisionist view of a strong 'old regime' England until internal collapse in 1828–32 is found in:

7 J. C. D. Clark, *English Society, 1688–1832* (Cambridge, 1985)

Among those historians whose reputations are assailed with the vitriol in Dr Clark's pen, but whose accounts of reform movements before 1789 nevertheless survive the experience, are:

8 G. F. E. Rudé, *Wilkes and Liberty* (Oxford, 1962)
9 I. R. Christie, *Wilkes, Wyvill and Reform* (London, 1962)
10 I. R. Christie, *Stress and Stability in Late Eighteenth-Century Britain* (Oxford, 1984)

There are now some excellent accounts of radicalism in the 1790s:

11 E. P. Thompson, *The Making of the English Working Class* (Penguin edn, London, 1968). Part I is essential reading on artisan radicalism and an important stimulus for:

12 H. T. Dickinson (ed.), *Britain and the French Revolution, 1789–1815* (London, 1989)
13 H. T. Dickinson, *British Radicalism and the French Revolution, 1789–1815* (Oxford, 1985) (Historical Association Pamphlet)
14 A. Goodwin, *The Friends of Liberty* (1979) – a thorough monograph

On the period between 1815 and 1832, the following texts all have useful further bibliographies:

15 D. G. Wright, *Popular Radicalism: The Working Class Experience, 1780–1880* (London, 1988)
16 E. J. Evans, *Britain before the Reform Act: Politics and Society, 1815–32* (Longman, 1989)
17 J. R. Dinwiddy. *From Luddism to the Reform Act* (Oxford, 1986) (Historical Association Pamphlet)
18 J. Belchem, *'Orator' Hunt: Henry Hunt and English Working Class Radicalism* (Oxford, 1985)

Two other *Lancaster Pamphlets*, published since the first edition of this book, provide useful linkages:

19 E. J. Evans, *Political Parties in Britain, 1783–1867* (London, 1985)
20 J. K. Walton, *The Second Reform Act* (London, 1987)

Two new biographies of Earl Grey have recently appeared:

21 E. A. Smith, *Lord Grey, 1764–1845* (Oxford 1990) – detailed and well-footnoted

22 J. W. Derry, *Charles, Earl Grey: Aristocratic Reformer* (Oxford, 1992) – readable but less weighty

Detailed texts on 1832 and its immediate aftermath include:

23 N. Gash, *Politics in the Age of Peel* (revised edn, London, 1977)
24 I. Newbould, *Whiggery and Reform, 1830–41* (London, 1990) – a useful corrective to Gash's view, especially on the Whigs
25 J. A. Phillips, *The Great Reform Bill in the Boroughs: English Electoral Behaviour, 1818–41* (Oxford, 1992)
26 P. Mandler, *Aristocratic Government in the Age of Reform: Whigs and Liberals, 1830–52* (Oxford, 1990)
27 J. A. Phillips, 'The many faces of reform: The Reform Bill and the electorate', *Parliamentary History*, Vol. 1 (1982), pp. 115–35
28 J. Vernon, *Politics and the People: A Study in English Political Culture, 1815–67* (Cambridge, 1993)

Two brief accounts of parliamentary reform are:

29 H. J. Hanham, *The Reformed Electoral System in Great Britain, 1832–1914* (London, 1968)
30 R. Stewart, *Party and Politics, 1830–52* (London, 1989), Chapter 3: 'British History in Perspective Series'

Textbooks which put the issues discussed here into wider context are:

31 E. J. Evans, *The Forging of the Modern State: Early Industrial Britain, 1783–1870* (London, 1983)
32 I. R. Christie, *Wars and Revolutions: Britain, 1760–1815* (London, 1982)
33 N. Gash, *Aristocracy and People, 1815–65* (London, 1979)
34 N. McCord, *British History, 1815–1906* (Oxford, 1991)
35 G. Williams and J. Ramsden, *Ruling Britannia: A Political History of Britain, 1688–1988* (London, 1990) – lively, but inevitably brief given the length of the period covered

A complete list of the changes brought about in 1832 (including the lists of disfranchised and enfranchised boroughs) is found in:

36 H. J. Hanham, *The Nineteenth-Century Constitution* (Cambridge, 1969), pp. 262–70

For a useful collection contemporary source material about the Reform Act crisis, see:

37 E. A. Smith, *Reform or Revolution?: A Diary of Reform in England, 1830–32* (Stroud, 1992)